The Reason Why We Sing

Function and Congregational Song in Different Musical Traditions

The Reason Why We Sing

Function and Congregational Song in Different Musical Traditions

Dr. Heather Josselyn-Cranson, OSL

OSL Publications
Ashland City TN

The Reason Why We Sing

Function and Congregational Song in Different Musical Traditions

ISBN: 978-1-878009-73-9

Produced and manufactured in the United States of America by

OSL Publications

The publishing ministry on The Order of Saint Luke
1002 Hunters Lane
Ashland City TN 37015

The Order of Saint Luke is a religious order dedicated to sacramental and liturgical scholarship, education and practice. The mission of the publishing ministry is to put into the hands of students and practitioners resources which have theological, historical, ecumenical and practical integrity.

CONTENTS

i

ACKNOWLEDGEMENTS

This work arose out of my classes with students studying music ministry at Northwestern College. I am grateful to these students for their willingness to explore and appreciate the breadth of Christian worship music in its variety of purpose as well as sound and style.

The cover art was designed specifically for this book by Emily Stokes, currently an Assistant Professor of Art at Northwestern College in Orange City, Iowa. She holds an MFA from Arizona State University and a BA from Wellesley College. Her visual work uses printmaking, drawing, painting, and digital imaging to construct narratives about her surroundings. The cover image is a three-run monotype using yellow, red, and blue inks.

Ron Anderson and Elise Eslinger each read through the manuscript for this book, contributing out of their wealth of knowledge, experience, and insight. They have made this a far better work, while the deficiencies that remain are mine alone.

I offer appreciation to Capital Music CMG, Cecilia Clemons, GIA, Hope Publishing, Sovereign Lifestyle Music, and Music Services (Vineyard USA) for permission to include copyrighted music and lyrics in this book.

DEDICATION

I would like to dedicate this volume, in profound gratitude, to Linda Clark, the James R. Houghton Scholar of Sacred Music at Boston University School of Theology for many years. Linda pushed her students to question not just what music means, but *how* it means. My scholarship, teaching, and practice owe much to her influence and encouragement.

CHAPTER 1 "THE POINT OF THE SINGING" FUNCTION IN THE CHURCH'S CONGREGATIONAL SONG

Someone asked the question,
"Why do we sing?
When we lift our hands to Jesus
What do we really mean?"[1]

What is music during the worship service supposed to *do*? Congregation members, pastors, and church musicians often assume that in order to sing well and faithfully, Christians must lift up their voices for the right reason. Musician and liturgical theologian Don Saliers speaks for this point of view when he writes that the "texts we sing and the musical forms we employ will flourish only so far as they faithfully serve the point of the singing."[2] Yet he does not state what that point is. How does music function in worship? Or, as Kirk Franklin asks, "Why do we sing?"

Many Christians believe that they know what church music ought to do. They may feel convinced that the role of music in church is the praise of God. They may think that music is what ties together sermon, scripture, and prayer into one cohesive unit. Others may see music as a catechesis of sorts: a chance to learn, understand, and

---

[1] Kirk Franklin, "Someone Asked the Question" in *The Faith We Sing* (Nashville: Abingdon Press, 2000), 2144.

[2] Don Saliers, *Worship and Spirituality* (Akron: OSL Publications, 1996), 21.

remember their faith though a poet's clever phrases and a composer's beautiful melody. Alternately, music may be what lifts the spirits and brings the mind to dwell on eternal things. Or music may be what allows the congregation to express its true feelings honestly and completely.

Since church leaders and musicians believe that music in worship must serve the right "point" in order to fulfill its purpose, we concern ourselves with discerning the right function for music in worship. And this search is curiously singular: we often assume there is only *one* correct role for music in church. Such an assumption gives us grounds for criticizing forms of music other than those we like and use. One person, for example, might assume that the role of music is to praise God. That person might reject examples of music that are sung *about* God rather than addressed *to* God, believing that music as praise should be a direct expression from the created to the Creator. Another person might believe that music serves to reflect the scriptural theme or sermon topic for the day. That person might feel frustration when encountering a body of music that is primarily doxological rather than thematic.

When discussing the differences of opinion regarding music in worship, a topic that occasionally descends into the "worship wars" of popular speech, we generally focus on musical taste, theological orientation, level of complexity, and relevance to contemporary culture. In other words, we assume that a Christian might prefer one piece or style of music over another based on how close it is to preferred secular musical styles, or what the text of the piece means, or how difficult it is. We forget that different understandings of the function of music in worship may have a great deal to do with one's dissatisfaction with various styles of music. In other words, a Christian may not like some music because it does not accomplish what he or she expects music to do in worship.

MANY REASONS FOR SINGING

I propose that there are not one but several roles for music in worship. These roles are manifested in various worshipping traditions. Different groups of Christians have used, and continue to use, music to serve different purposes within the format of Christian worship. Much of this difference has arisen out of particular historical circumstances. A time of doctrinal confusion, for example, may yield congregational music with catechetical properties, while a time of emphasis on evangelism may foster music with invitational and testimonial characteristics.

Often, the role of music within one style is not completely absent from the worship of another style, but merely served through prayer, or preaching, or individual testimony rather than singing. For example, a tradition of worship that uses music as praise does not entirely neglect the catechetical or faith formation aspect of worship, but may relegate that function to the scripture reading or sermon instead of the congregation's song. One might find this situation at an evangelical church, where music probably includes popular contemporary songs of praise by Chris Tomlin or Matt Redman, songs which revel in the joy of praising God instead of delineating a theological understanding of who God is. Yet the congregation participates in a time of learning about who God is when well-worn bibles are pulled out, scripture is expounded, and faith is formed through the sermon. Likewise, a congregation in which music serves as catechesis, where the Gloria and the Creed are sung each week, may not use its singing to lament, protest, or otherwise engage in "truth-telling" about the world. Instead, this congregation may offer such truths during the time of

3

prayer, when the intersection of faith and social or political concerns is raised in spoken rather than sung form.

This variety of intentions in using music can be a source of great misunderstanding. Anyone moving from one worship tradition to another is likely to stumble over new assumptions about what music should accomplish and how it should be used. The examples mentioned above, of a Christian who wants to sing *to* God rather than *about* God, or of the music leader who encounters music collections with little more than "Adoration and Praise" in the subject index, demonstrate the typical frustrations that arise when coming upon new expectations about the role of music. These misunderstandings can be particularly challenging since music affects people deeply, engaging thought, emotions, memories, and the lived practice of meeting God in worship week after week. Despite the possibilities for conflict, however, having such diverse roles for worship music is also a blessing for the Church.

In particular, this variety can be a blessing because the way that Christians worship, especially including their singing, affects the way that they understand God. Christians from one tradition, for example, might value an orthodox doctrinal and theological understanding of God. This value would be reinforced and heightened through objective or didactic music for worship, including texts such as the Nicene Creed or the *Te Deum* that describe the God of Abraham, Isaac, and Jacob as found in scripture and Church tradition. Those from another tradition may stress the use of spiritual disciplines to come into the presence of God, and the words sung by that congregation might serve as a sung *lectio divina*, set to simple melodies that can be repeated meditatively. These songs, including "Come and Fill our Hearts with Your Peace" or O Lord, Hear My Prayer" from the Taizé tradition, might hint at a God as near to us as our own breath, a God who speaks in quiet and stillness. A third tradition might emphasize utter honesty in coming before the Lord, the

God who abides in and through all of the struggles of human existence. The adherents of this tradition may choose songs of lament and solidarity, such as "Go Down, Moses" or "I Want Jesus to Walk with Me," to stand with God on the side of the poor and protest boldly those things that obstruct the Kingdom of God. In these examples, each tradition emphasizes one facet of the nature of God, and of our relationship with God. But God is multi-faceted, and limited human traditions can easily narrow the approach to God, and even the person of God, in the eyes of worshipping Christians.

Church musicians and all who lead congregational worship, therefore, need to understand the wealth of musical traditions in the church, not only in order to perform in a variety of styles but in order to comprehend what various congregations intend to do when they sing. With such a broad understanding of the different functions of music in place, the worship leader or musician can affirm each congregation's practices while slowly and lovingly introducing new styles of music, new roles for singing, and ultimately new images of God to the congregation. Such a musician could help the "catechetical music" church, mentioned in the example above, encounter and accept God's openness to honest lament through song. This minister of music could find orthodox and formative theological texts to assist the "spiritual disciplines" church in expanding its understanding of the One who so loved the world. And this wise musician could introduce texts of simple contemplation to remind the "honest lament" church that the Lord who values the deepest cries of the heart also encourages us to draw close in quiet, meditative presence.

Problems with, and Examples of, Variety

It may be difficult for some to allow a variety of valid purposes for music in the context of Christian worship. Having been formed in our faith in a church that proclaims, "one Lord, one faith, one baptism,"[3] we may expect to find "the [one] point of the singing," and not "the points." Yet the Christian scriptures show a remarkable tolerance for and even appreciation of diversity and plurality. The book of Psalms, for example, includes thanksgivings, laments, praises, and wisdom literature within its canon of prayer, making room for expressions of the full range of human emotion in a variety of genres.

In the New Testament, we find that the first Christians wrestled with the question of circumcision and Jewish food laws, ultimately deciding that while some believers may keep fast to the traditions of their Jewish ancestors, the Gentile converts were not required to do so. Thus Peter and Paul entered into two different ministries for two separate communities (Acts 10-11, 15). The Apostle Paul wrote to the Church in Corinth that the Holy Spirit gives a variety of gifts that are manifested in different people uniquely (1 Corinthians 12). To that same community, he also points out that both eating food offered to idols and abstaining from such food are valid and faithful choices, so long as concern for others influences one's decision (1 Corinthians 8). Truly, the "one faith" seems to have been always open to a variety of manifestations.

Likewise, there has been breadth in understanding the role of music in worship throughout the history of the Christian Church. Often the same theologian or leader will describe one purpose for singing in

---

[3] Ephesians 4:5

one place, only to imply or mandate another function of worship in another place. Such variety obtains even in the Bible.

The song of the angels, elders, and four living creatures described in Revelation 7:11-12 is one of joyous praise: "Blessing and glory and wisdom and thanksgiving and honor and power and might be to our God forever and ever!" Yet Paul, in his letter to the Colossians, couches his musical instructions to that congregation in terms relating to unity and fellowship. Here, singing "psalms, hymns, and spiritual songs" (Col 3:16) seems to be part and parcel of bearing with one another, forgiving each other, (verse 13) and binding all things together in love (verse 14). Paul and Silas' hymn-singing while in prison (Acts 16:25) implies yet another purpose: building up the apostles' faith and providing comfort in the face of persecution. Calvin Stapert, in his volume on early Christian ideas about music, finds two prominent and complementary roles for music in the New Testament: rejoicing and crying for mercy.[4] He also identifies allusions to other roles for music, including responding to the Word of Christ and evangelization.[5]

This variety of acceptable functions for music in worship did not end after the New Testament was codified. Clement of Alexandria, like many thinkers of his day, found in music the power to mold emotions and even behavior. But he also identified a Eucharistic, or thanksgiving, quality to Christian music-making. As Stapert summarizes, Clement believed that "Christians should want to make noble music not only to shape noble character, though they should not ignore that aspect

---

[4] Calvin R. Stapert, *A New Song for an Old World: Musical Thought in the Early Church* (Grand Rapids: Eerdmans, 2007), 16-17.

[5] Ibid., 20-22.

of music; but more fundamentally, Christians make music because they are thankful."[6]

John Chrysostom refers to the character-shaping feature of music in a more practical way in his *Exposition of Psalm XLI*, where he lays this role alongside yet another purpose for singing. While singing the Psalms leads to "much of value, much utility, much sanctity, and every inducement to philosophy, for the words purify the mind and the Holy Spirit descends swiftly on the mind of the singer," Chrysostom also recognizes that "nothing so uplifts the mind, giving it wings and freeing it from the earth," as music.[7] Therefore, he concludes that "God established the psalms, in order that singing might be both a pleasure and a help."[8]

Looking particularly at psalmody, scholar Paul Bradshaw has recently identified six different way that early Christian communities used psalm singing: as Christological prophecy, as summary of Scripture, as hymns, as praise, as penance, and as intercession. He then distinguishes between the first three functions, which he believes depend primarily on the content of the texts of the psalms, and the last three, which depend instead on the intentions of the one praying or singing. For example, one might offer to God the singing of a fixed number of psalms as an act of penance, regardless of the words of the psalms being sung. Bradshaw's brief inquiry into purpose in the ancient Christian use of psalmody provides abundant examples of how various

---

[6] Ibid., 57.

[7] John Chrysostom, *Exposition of Psalm XLI*, ed. Oliver Strunk, *Source Readings in Music History* (New York: Norton, 1950), 67-68.

[8] Ibid.

Christian communities engaged in the same practice, singing the psalms, yet understood the point of that practice entirely differently.[9]

The Reformers likewise wrestled with the proper role for music within new forms for worship. John Calvin, drawing on his understanding of scriptures as well as his reading of Plato, instructed his readers that music serves as a form of prayer, incites people to praise their creator, molds the characters of those who sing, and recreates or refreshes the congregation through the pleasure of creating sound.[10] In the eighteenth century, John Wesley also realized the power of singing in worship, and he tried to harness and explain that power within the movement he and his brother began. Like Calvin, Wesley was familiar with Greek musical thought, however he highlighted yet a different role for music to fill. He favored quick, vigorous singing, which "tends to awake and enliven the soul."[11]

Just as these Christian leaders, thinkers, evangelists and authors have found many acceptable and beneficial purposes for music, modern-day Christians can also recognize the multitude of ways in which music serves God and the Church within the context of worship.

---

[9] Paul Bradshaw, *Reconstructing Early Christian Worship* (Collegeville, Minnesota: Liturgical Press, 2010), 117-131.

[10] John Calvin, "Foreword to the Genevan Psalter," translated and edited by Oliver Strunk, in *Source Readings in Music History* (New York: Norton, 1950), 346.

[11] Carlton R. Young, *Music of the Heart: John and Charles Wesley on Music and Musicians* (Carol Stream, IL: Hope Publishing, 1995), 65. On Wesley and Greek musical thought, see 84-93.

Attention to the Role of Music in Recent Scholarship

Several scholars of music in the church have addressed the topic of function within a congregation's musical practices. In 1988, Lutheran musician and scholar Paul Westermeyer published *The Church Musician*, a helpful work on the nature of leading congregational music-making which interweaves the practical and the theological in a graceful and faithful way. Westermeyer intended to write for church leaders, whether members of worship committees or ordained pastors, as well as for the musicians who work alongside these leaders. Although Westermeyer's personal history, as a trained organist and an informed Lutheran, influences the work, his proclivity for seeing the larger picture and finding fundamental principles means that his work can be easily "translated" by the reader to any denominational setting or musical style.

In Chapter 4 of *The Church Musician*, Westermeyer suggests that the church musician's job is to ensure five roles for the congregation's song: praising God, lifting up prayer, proclaiming the gospel, sharing the story of the Church, and embodying a gift from God.[12] These tasks are not all equally clear. While many Christians would recognize and agree that they can praise God as well as pray to God through song, Westermeyer admits that proclamation is a "less obvious aspect" of what music in worship can do. His descriptions of proclamation and story-telling leave some confusion as to how these roles differ from one another. And music as gift seems unequal to the other roles; even the grammatical shift from the verbs "praise" and "proclaim" to the noun "gift" signals that this one role is different from the others. Later in his

---

[12] Paul Westermeyer, *The Church Musician*, 2nd ed (Minneapolis: Augsburg Fortress, 1997), 31-36.

description, Westermeyer hints that as gift, music lets the congregation receive refreshment from God. In any case, these five categories, while still raising some questions, provide one way for church leaders and ministers of music to assess the breadth of their congregational music.

Miriam Therese Winter, a scholar of Catholic liturgy and music, took an entirely different tack in her book *Why Sing? Toward a Theology of Catholic Church Music.* Although the resulting work is as deeply and faithfully reasoned and as desirous of helping modern day church musicians as was Westermeyer's, Winter's post-Vatican Catholic context led her on a different route. For Winter, the key issue was that "no theology of Roman Catholic Church music exists to serve as a guide for the interpretation and implementation of the directives of Vatican II."[13] While her search for such a theology led her to mine an inexhaustible number of papal letters, council documents, and pieces of liturgical legislation, not to mention secondary sources, her ultimate goal was to elucidate Church teachings so that local musicians may serve their congregations with pastoral sensitivity and musical excellence. While clearly written for Roman Catholics, Winter's work sheds light on much of the shared Christian history of employing music in worship, and thus may be of interest to Protestant students of church music, too.

After wading through centuries of Church teaching, Winter concludes that music in the context of worship serves as an offering to God, an experience which ministers to and involves the entire congregation, and a sign and symbol of love for God which can transform each Christian.[14] These are interesting conclusions, worthy of

---

[13] Miriam Therese Winter, *Why Sing? Toward a Theology of Catholic Church Music* (Washington, DC: The Pastoral Press, 1984), 7.

[14] Ibid., 230-231.

discussion. First, music is an offering to God because it is an integral part of the "unbloody" sacrifice of the Mass, which is the offering of both priest and congregation. Yet Winter then states that the singing of the Divine Office is also an offering, without explaining the relationship of sacrifice to that non-sacramental form of worship. She also states that song is the "Church's perfect prayer of praise" when it is "perfectly rendered" and "sung precisely as prescribed by those duly appointed." Such intimations that human beings can achieve perfection, in music or in any realm, and that our perfection is what makes our song pleasing to God are troubling, to say the least.

More familiar, and comfortable, to many church musicians is Winter's argument that music both involves (or should involve) the whole congregation and ministers to that congregation. She locates this ministry in singing, which "connects [people] with each other, mediates the Word of Life to an assembly of believers, [and] puts the power of the liturgical event in touch with human need."[15] Finally, as music is a symbol of "a commitment in faith," it not only expresses that faith but changes the singer.   Song, according to Winter, "is a tool of transformation, capable of effecting a conversion of the heart."[16] But these purposes for music in worship are only a sideline on Winter's quest for a comprehensive theology of church music, and so she moves on to other topics without exploring the nuances of each of these points.

Presbyterian pastor and scholar William S. Smith published his work on church music, *Joyful Noise: A Guide to Music in the Church for Pastors and Musicians*, in 2007. In many respects, Smith aims to create what Paul Westermeyer accomplished with *The Church Musician* and

---

[15] Ibid., 231.

[16] Ibid.

present a book that will be of practical help to those working in the field of music ministry. Including chapters on acoustics and architecture, planning and choosing music, the role of instruments in worship, and other topics, the author tries to cover broadly the various facets of what church musicians do and how they think about it. Yet where Westermeyer strives to state broad principles that would speak to any congregational situation, Smith feels firmly and cheerfully committed to congregations with hymnals, organs, choirs, and other hallmarks of "traditional" worship. He sequesters material on "contemporary" worship into one chapter, a decision that confirms Smith's discomfort with this style. Such an approach feels anachronistic in an age of unparalleled diversity in Christian approaches to worship.

Smith tackles the topic of musical function head-on in the first chapter of his book. He states that music's role in worship is to serve the liturgy by both interpreting and enhancing the emotional power of the liturgy itself.[17] Smith offers a more phenomenological approach to the question in his second chapter, by providing a list of outcomes that can or should happen when the congregation sings. He includes such results as praising, incorporating the physical body into worship, broadening our images of God, increasing our desire to worship, praying, building the faith of the congregation, ensuring theological balance in the Church's emphases, testing theology, motivating singers to live their faith, fostering unity within the congregation and among Christians of all times and places, building one another up, and evangelizing.[18] This list easily leads one to hold church music in greater esteem, even while

---

[17] William S. Smith, *Joyful Noise: A Guide to Music in the Church for Pastors and Musicians* (Franklin, Tennessee: Providence House Publishers, 2007), 15-17.

[18] Ibid., 22-50.

recognizing that not all of these outcomes obtain in every congregation. Yet the multiplicity of benefits described by the author can also distract the reader from Smith's earlier point: that music is the humble servant of the liturgy, and fulfills its role best when it assists that liturgy through interpretation or amplification of emotional resonance.

The work of Smith, Winter, and Westermeyer shares several commonalities. First, while these glimpses into how congregational singing ought to function are helpful, they often describe idealized goals rather than an actual state of affairs in a particular local congregation.[19] Certainly goals are helpful, especially to church musicians and other leaders who seek to create a healthy and God-honoring musical life within the church. Yet to describe something that may happen or ought to happen to often to misinterpret, or simply to ignore, what is, in fact, happening. In addition to describing hypothetical or ideal scenarios, it is also important to look at music (including texts, tunes, the way these are used, their placement within the service and other practices associated with music-making in worship) as it happens weekly in a variety of real congregations.

Secondly, all three authors affirm that music can, and should, fulfill a variety of roles within worship. Westermeyer, for example, asserts that a healthy music program must include story-telling as well as prayer, proclamation as well as praise. Smith goes even further in enumerating the ways in which music can serve the congregation. I

---

[19] Another, briefer, glimpse into musical function is present in Steven R. Janco's article "From Stylistic Stalemate to Focus on Function," *Liturgy* 24, no. 4 (2009): 48-54. Janco looks at four functions of the entrance song within the Roman Catholic Mass; he suggests that focusing on function, as he does, might help church musicians avoid "stumbling blocks" that frequently occur in conversations, or arguments, concerning musical style. Janco briefly mentions, but does not explore, the idea that certain styles of music are more aligned with particular liturgical functions than others.

agree with Westermeyer, Winter, and Smith that music functions in many ways. Yet in the congregations I have observed, I have found that often one function seems favored above the others. Furthermore, I believe that which music function the congregation favors depends in large part upon the worship and musical style generally employed. None of the above-mentioned authors correlate musical styles with emphases on particular functions within their lists. Neither Westermeyer, Winter, nor Smith intended to investigate or compare a variety of worship styles. I think, however, that such a comparison, paying careful attention to musical function and to stylistic differences, could be revealing.

It is my contention that various musical traditions within the Church have gradually accented certain roles for music and minimized others. Sometimes these accents are clearly evident, as in the contemporary musical repertoire known as "praise and worship." Such a tradition obviously expects that its music should function doxologically. In other cases, these roles are more subtle. Songs in the Taizé tradition, for example, are often called chants or prayers, yet their calming and repetitive nature reminds one strongly of the spiritual disciplines. This study will explore the connections between musical style and musical purpose as these interact in various modern-day congregational traditions.

CLASSIFICATION SYSTEMS FOR MUSIC AND WORSHIP

In order to discuss different functions for music within different traditions, we must provide a taxonomy, or system of classification, for these differences. Several such taxonomies have been suggested by scholars of worship and church music. The most radical might be that of Lester Ruth, who proposes that scholars abandon terms like "liturgical,"

15

"blended," "contemporary," and "traditional" in favor of a new system based on two continua. The first continuum addresses content: "personal-story" churches primarily center on "themes of particular interest to the worshipers," while "cosmic-story" churches primarily lift up narratives of God's saving actions throughout human history.[20] Ruth's second continuum addresses worship structure: worship services can be organized by and focused on music, Word/preaching, or Sacrament. According to Ruth, "one of these three is usually the normal means by which a congregation assesses God's presence in worship or believes that God is made present in worship."[21]

As inventive and thought-provoking as Ruth's concept is, his second continuum assumes that certain traditions value music more than others, a problematic supposition for a study of the music of many different styles of worship, each of which values music for different reasons. Likewise, since this classification addresses differences in worship rather than music specifically, it may leave some musical distinctions behind. A suburban, main-line congregation may fit into the "cosmic-story," Word/preaching-organized category, as might an urban, African-American congregation. Yet these two congregations probably sing different repertoires of music and may well expect this music to function in different ways.

C. Michael Hawn provides another taxonomy focusing on contemporary North American worship music, based on an extensive study of hymnals from the past few decades. He identifies seven

---

[20] Lester Ruth, "A Rose by Any Other Name: Attempts at Classifying North American Protestant Worship," in *The Conviction of Things Not Seen: Currents in Protestant Christianity in the Twenty-First Century*, ed. Todd E. Johnson (Grand Rapids: Brazos Press, 2002), 47.

[21] Ibid., 48.

"streams of congregational song:" Roman Catholic liturgical renewal hymnody, Protestant contemporary classical hymnody, African American spirituals and gospel songs, revival/gospel songs, folk song influences, Pentecostal songs, and global and ecumenical song forms.[22] Such a scheme proves extremely helpful in identifying the sources and development of various styles of singing in worship. As Hawn himself admits, however, he is more interested in the source of these streams than the ways that various congregations recombine them in their weekly worship. His categories serve as better descriptors of what music has been produced for congregational use than what individual congregations select and use in their weekly worship. Many congregations borrow from more than one of these "streams" in building a repertoire of music for worship. Hawn also does not address the question of function or purpose in his study.

Another classification of worship styles, rather than strictly musical genres, comes from Paul Basden's *Exploring the Worship Spectrum*. Basden sorts worship patterns into six genres: Formal-Liturgical, Traditional Hymn-Based, Contemporary Music-Driven, Charismatic, Blended, and Emerging. [23] These categories echo commonly-used contemporary language for describing worship in congregations. Yet they point to differences in worship as a whole rather than music in particular, and they cannot in every case be mapped easily onto musical styles. There is no emerging repertoire of church music, for example; emerging congregations are marked by how

---

[22] C. Michael Hawn, "Streams of Song: An overview of congregational song in the twenty-first century," in *The Hymn*, vol. 61, no.1, Winter 2010, 16-26. Hawn has also published his findings in a more extensive form in *New Songs of Celebration Render: Congregational Song in the Twenty-First Century* (Chicago: GIA, 2013).

[23] Paul Basden, ed., *Exploring the Worship Spectrum* (Grand Rapids: Zondervan, 2004).

they use music eclectically and locally rather than by what music they use. Yet Basden's taxonomy is rooted in descriptions of how various congregations put musical and liturgical ideas and artifacts into practice, rather than in the origins of those artifacts and ideas.

The Structure of This Book

For the purposes of this study, we will borrow those categories from Hawn and Basden that seem most descriptive of what various congregations sing each week in order to create a taxonomy of musical function in worship. We will examine liturgical worshipping traditions that use music as *catechesis* in understanding the Christian faith. We will explore the use of hymns as *vehicles for congregational response* in hymn-singing traditions. We will investigate the *testimonial* function of the gospel song that arose in nineteenth-century America and continues in popularity. Then we will turn to the collection of praise and worship music used *doxologically* by what is often referred to as the "contemporary" church. Next we will study the music of two diverse worshipping practices: the quiet chant of Taizé and the improvisatory choruses of the charismatic tradition, both of which serve as a sung *spiritual discipline*. Finally, we will consider the range of spirituals and gospels used to *speak truth through lament and protest* in the African-American Church.

Each chapter of this work will investigate one of the categories of music above. For each musical repertoire, we will explore the historical roots of this form of music and worship. Using several examples, we will identify the way in which the texts of this body of music function in worship as well as the ways in which the aural components of the style assist that function. Then, we will look for Biblical traces of both practices of and attitudes toward worship and

18

music that shed some light on this way of using music. Next, we will address the criticism that each genre of church music has faced. Finally, we will suggest ways in which practitioners of other music and worship styles might incorporate elements of this function into their own congregational worship.

Any system of classification contains weaknesses, since categories are only imperfectly descriptive and not absolutely proscriptive. Music, in particular, is always more varied and subtle than the limited number of categories to which it is assigned. Making generalizations, as this study does, always leaves one open to the charge that certain examples lie outside the simplified overview provided. Not all hymns, for example, respond directly to scripture, sermon, or the other elements of worship. Songs of praise can be found in Taizé prayer as well as in liturgical forms of worship, while Contemporary Worship Music does not always center on the praise of God. But whereas these categories and statements of musical function are generalizations, they are useful in highlighting important trends within each tradition. If understood as common practices rather than impermeable divisions, they may be helpful to anyone interested in understanding the varieties of music and worship present in American churches today, and the ways this music is employed.

The limited number of categories used in this study also excludes some forms of singing. Hawn's category of global songs has not been included, primarily because extremely few North American congregations use these songs as their principal musical diet. Additionally, global praise comes from a multitude of cultural backgrounds, and it would be simplistic to presume that each of these shares the same ideas about how music should function in the context of worship. Likewise, I have not included genres used less frequently in

American worship, such as Christian metal, screamo, bluegrass, hip-hop, and others.

Finally, this study focuses on worship music that is intended primarily for congregational singing. Although instrumental music, choral anthems, and solo works can be a great blessing to the congregation's worship, I will concentrate on what the congregation intends to do when it participates vocally in music.

It is my hope that this exploration of "the point[s] of the singing" will help congregations gain a better understanding of their worship traditions; assist worship leaders in understanding the assumptions behind their congregations' musical practices; aid music leaders in serving a wider variety of congregations with knowledge and confidence; and call all the people of God to expand their awareness of the many ways to use music in a worshipful encounter with their Creator.

CHAPTER 2: SINGING IN THE FORMAL-LITURGICAL TRADITION
SONG AS CATECHESIS

By singing the doxology in worship Sunday after Sunday we learn to interpret our world in such a way that we see it as good and offer praise to God for this goodness. We learn that God is the source of all goodness, the one from whom blessings flow. Likewise, the doxology places us within a broad cosmic context in which all creatures praise God. Humanity finds its place within a vast created order that includes everything from angels to cosmic dust, and each of these creatures exists to glorify God.

We may not think about these things each time we sing the doxology; we may not unpack its meaning and remind ourselves of these truths, but it works its way into our souls anyway. The doxology becomes part of us, and as a result we become doxological beings. We are not simply people whose minds have grasped the truths the doxology teaches us: we are people whose hearts have been changed by that truth.[24]

We have put this music on the living and holy Word of God in order to sing, praise, and honor it. We want the beautiful art of music to be properly used to serve her dear Creator and his Christians. He is thereby praised and honored and we are made better and stronger in faith when his holy Word is impressed on our hearts by sweet music. God the Father with Son and Holy Spirit grant us this, Amen.[25]

In the dualistic world of the "worship wars," it often seems that all that is not a hymn is contemporary, and all that is not played by a

---

[24] Kendra G. Hotz and Matthew T. Mathews, *Shaping the Christian Life: Worship and the Religious Affections* (Louisville: Westminster John Knox Press, 2006), 3.

[25] Martin Luther, "Preface to the Burial Hymns," in *Liturgy and Hymns*, ed. Ulrich S. Leupold; trans. Paul Zeller Strodach; vol. 53 of *Luther's Works*, American Edition, ed. Jaroslav Pelikan and Helmut T. Lehmann, (Philadelphia: Fortress, 1965), 328.

band is a traditional hymn. Yet the first style or use of music that we will examine falls outside of these two options. Paul Zahl, a systematic theologian and Episcopal priest who argues on behalf of the style or structure of service that uses music in this way, calls this formal-liturgical worship. Zahl defines this style as "Bible-based verticality... [unequaled] for taking you outside your problems and also bringing you back to them a renewed person, better able to cope and to endure... prescribed worship, service that is required for a given occasion."[26] Timothy Quill, a voice from the Lutheran perspective, labels this style "liturgical," and posits that "the traditional Liturgy looks the way it does for theological reasons... [it] reflects a biblical, Trinitarian, Christological, sacramental, and eschatological character."[27] Whatever we call it, this form of worship uses music to recite and repeat core texts of worship, often including creeds, psalms, prayers, scripture, and historic texts of praise. The congregation sings these core texts week after week, and they are required elements that constitute the worship service itself. Some of these core texts are familiar to many Christians, such as the Lord's Prayer (Our Father). Others may be known only to congregations that regularly include them, such as the Agnus Dei (Lamb of God) or the Memorial Acclamation. Thus in the formal-liturgical style of worship, music is generally used to clothe many of the verbal elements that make

---

[26] Paul Zahl, "Formal-Liturgical Worship," in *Exploring the Worship Spectrum: 6 Views, ed.* Paul A. Basden, (Grand Rapids: Zondervan, 2004), 23. Later on, Zahl elaborates on what "Bible-based verticality" means: "It is transcendent before it is horizontal... This means that it is not pastor- or preacher-centered. It is, or ought to be, Word-centered... formal-liturgical worship depends on its fidelity to the Bible understanding of God, Christ, and us" (24-27).

[27] Timothy C. J. Quill, "Liturgical Worship," in *Perspectives on Christian Worship: 5 Views*, ed. J. Matthew Pinson (Nashville: B&H Academic, 2009), 81.

up the time of worship, rather than added, in the form of hymn or song, before or after these core texts.[28]

The formal-liturgical style is frequently found in Roman Catholic, Episcopal, and Lutheran congregations. These denominations have relatively fixed structures for worship that adhere more or less closely to a long-lived historical pattern of Christian worship. A desire for fidelity to ancient and widespread forms of Christian worship encourages these denominations to use many early Christian core texts, such as creeds, psalms, and historic prayers. This adherence to older patterns of worship also ensures great similarity between the worship services of these denominations. Thus, a Roman Catholic may find an Episcopal service of Holy Eucharist quite familiar, while an Episcopalian would easily follow along when attending a Lutheran Holy Communion liturgy. While the melodies used to sing core texts in each denomination may be different, the core texts themselves remain remarkably consistent.

Some other mainline churches also incorporate elements of this style, whether by using sung doxologies or communion responses, including a creed spoken or sung weekly, offering the Gloria Patri at some point during worship, or limiting singing to a proscribed group of selections which are considered proper for worship: psalms, the ordinary of the mass, or other service music. While a minority of denominations strictly follow a formal-liturgical approach to music and

---

[28] Although the primary use of music within the formal-liturgical style is found in the singing of the core texts described above, formal-liturgical congregations may also include hymn-singing in their worship services. Yet hymns are usually added to the structure of formal-liturgical worship as an optional elaboration, while the core texts are obligatory parts of the service. For simplicity, I will limit the discussion in this chapter to the singing of those core texts, while hymn-singing will be examined separately in the next chapter.

worship, the use of core texts, repeated week after week, is surprisingly common.

THE HISTORY OF MUSIC IN THE FORMAL LITURGICAL STYLE

This style is possibly the most overtly "historical" style of worship, offering obvious evidence of its ties to the past. The structure of formal-liturgical worship is based around the ancient four-fold Christian worship pattern of greeting, word, sacrament, and sending forth.[29] The particular texts that make up the liturgy, which can be spoken, chanted, or sung in this style, often include the ordinary of the mass: five unchanging texts which are used at each service of word and table and which are prayed or proclaimed, often in song, by the entire congregation. The Kyrie ("Lord have mercy, Christ have mercy, Lord have mercy"), the Gloria ("Glory to God in the highest..."), the Credo, or Nicene Creed ("I believe in one God..."), the Sanctus ("Holy, Holy, Holy..."), and the Agnus Dei ("Lamb of God, who takes away the sins of the world...") are these quintessential core texts. Other repeated texts also exhibit the spirit of formal-liturgical sung worship. These include but are not limited to the Lord's Prayer, the Amen at the end of other prayers, congregational responses within the Eucharistic prayer in addition to the Sanctus[30], and the psalms. But where did the idea of a

---

[29] This structure can be found in many places, but one can read a fuller description of it in chapter 3 of Robert Webber's *Worship is a Verb*, (Waco: Word Books, 1985), 47-66.

[30] While the Sanctus quickly became a wide-spread congregational component of most Eucharistic prayers, other congregational responses arose which featured more rarely. Some of these responses are still used by various worshipping traditions today, and they include the Memorial Acclamation (which first appeared "Your death, Lord, we proclaim and your resurrection we confess," but now is often used in the third

fixed core of prayers and praises originate, and how did music come to be involved with such a way or worshipping?

One finds the practice of using fixed forms for singing and prayer in worship very early in the history of Christian liturgy. Many scholars think the first Eucharistic prayers derived from the *Kiddush* and the *Birkat ha-mazon*, blessings surrounding meal times within the Jewish tradition.[31] Others find that these prayers descended from the *Yotzer*, a blessing found in forms of Jewish morning prayer.[32] In either case, these fixed communal prayers are thought to have been typically chanted or sung in ancient Jewish practice.[33] There is every reason to believe that the early Christians, rooted in Jewish culture and liturgical practice, would likewise chant or sing the new communal prayers that grew out of these prayer forms.

Justin Martyr, in his writings of the second century, offers early testimony to some fixed elements in Christian worship. He documents

_____

person: "Christ has died, Christ has risen, Christ will come again") and the phrase "We hymn you, we bless you, we give you thanks, O Lord and we pray to you, our God." These congregational responses have attained some familiarity in some traditions, but they were not part of the ordinary of the mass as it appeared throughout much of Christian history. One can note the appearance of these phrases, as well as others, in R. C. D. Jasper and G. J. Cuming, eds, *Prayers of the Eucharist: Early and Reformed*, 2nd ed. (New York: Oxford University Press, 1980).

[31] Lucien Deiss, *Springtime of the Liturgy*, Matthew J. O'Connell, trans., (Collegeville, Minnesota: Liturgical Press, 1979), 4-9.

[32] Paul F. Bradshaw, *Reconstructing Early Christian Worship* (Collegeville, MN: Liturgical Press, 2009), 38-39. While Bradshaw himself hesitates to draw such explicit lines of derivation, he writes that Christian Eucharistic prayers "ultimately [have] their origin in Jewish meal prayers" (52).

[33] Alfred Sendry, *Music in Ancient Israel* (New York: Philosophical Library, 1969), 159-260. On singing at meal times, see particularly 174-175.

the congregation's unison offering of the "Amen" in both weekly worship and at baptismal services.[34] Sometime later, the *Apostolic Tradition* presents a common dialogue shared by priests and congregations at the beginning of the Eucharistic prayers:

> -The Lord be with all of you.
> May he be with your spirit.
> -Lift up your hearts.
> We have [them] with the Lord our God.
> -Let us give thanks to the Lord.
> It is right and a just thing.[35]

The five sections of the ordinary of the mass, core texts that influence Christian worship in many traditions to this day, were incorporated into liturgical practice slightly later. The Kyrie, a three-fold prayer for mercy, was described by a Christian pilgrim to Jerusalem at the end of the fourth century. This prayer served as a communal response to petitions offered by a leader. By the sixth century, the Kyrie stood at the beginning of the weekly worship service, as it does to this day in many traditions.[36] Over the course of time, the leader's petitions

---

[34] Deiss, 92-93.

[35] Paul F. Bradshaw, Maxwell E. Johnson, and L. Edward Phillips, *The Apostolic Constitution: A Commentary* (Minneapolis: Fortress Press, 2002), 38. The various linguistic sources for this text offer slight variances on the exact phrasing of this opening dialogue; I have included the Ethiopic version above. Liturgical scholars continue to disagree over the author, provenance, and date of the *Apostolic Tradition*. The authors of this edition have posited that the text is a compilation of material from several sources and communities, possibly ranging in date from the second to the fourth centuries (14). At any rate, other sources describing early Christian worship also include mention of a similar opening dialogue (43).

[36] Joseph A. Jungmann, *The Mass of the Roman Rite: Its Origins and Development*, vol. 1, Francis A. Brunner, trans., (New York: Benziger Brothers, 1951; replica edition Allen, Texas: Christian Classics, 1986), 334-336.

were eliminated, leaving only the sung response as a congregational prayer for mercy. Likewise, as musical forms grew in complexity, the *schola* or choir began to take over the people's role in singing this prayer for mercy. Kyrie melodies of great length and beauty were composed for such trained choirs, and these ornate compositions prevented ordinary Christians from participating in the song. Yet some scholars, at least, believe that in churches further removed from the example and authority of Rome, the entire congregation continued to sing a simple and repetitive Kyrie as in the past.[37]

The Gloria, also called the Greater Doxology, stems from the song of the angels in Luke 2:14, although it grew to incorporate an extended creedal statement about the identity of Christ. At first, this joyful outburst of praise was limited to celebrations of great pomp, but by the eleventh century, it was used on all Sundays and feast days, except during penitential seasons such as Advent and Lent. Medieval liturgical author Amalarius of Metz described the way in which first one angel, then a host of angels appeared to the shepherds in Luke 2, commenting that "In this same way one priest begins and the entire church echoes praise to God."[38] The Gloria, like the Kyrie, became a song for the musically-trained leaders of the mass in larger churches, while smaller and more remote congregations continued to intone or recite the earlier and simpler Gloria melodies.[39]

Despite its name, the Nicene Creed was codified at the Council of Chalcedon in 451, not the fourth-century Council of Nicaea. The creed was not, however, immediately used in weekly worship. At first

---

[37] Ibid., 342-343.

[38] Ibid., 356-358, translation mine.

[39] Ibid., 358-359.

employed only at baptisms, this statement of belief crept into corporate worship over the next several centuries, particularly in response to heresies.[40] The length of the creedal statement, and the fact that it remained in Latin among all Western Christians until the sixteenth century (and among many Western Christians until the 1960's), has at times proved a stumbling block to its musical performance by the whole congregation. Yet the simple melodies preserved in notation for the Credo testify to the Church's goal of having the whole congregation join in this profession of faith, even if such a goal was not always achieved.[41]

The Sanctus is "a reminder that the earthly church should take part in the heavenly singing... All the people join in singing the Sanctus – that was taken for granted in ancient Christian times."[42] The Apostolic Constitutions of the late 4th century instruct that all the people should join in the Sanctus text, which comes from Isaiah 6:3 and Mark 11:9 and shares similarities with Revelation 4:8.[43] These verses served as a communal song of praise at the celebration of the Lord's Supper for centuries, until the rise of polyphony in the high middle ages.[44] As

---

[40] Ibid., 462-470. Also Peter G. Cobb, "The Liturgy of the Word in the Early Church" in *The Study of Liturgy*, revised ed., eds. Cheslyn Jones, Geoffrey Wainwright, Edward Yarnold, and Paul Bradshaw (New York: Oxford University Press, 1992), 228.

[41] Jungmann, 472-473. Cobb agrees with Jungmann that the Nicene Creed was certainly sung by Western Christians, although notes that it was spoken, not sung, in the Byzantine Liturgy employed among Eastern Christians.

[42] Ibid., vol 2, 128.

[43] Deiss, 232, Scholars often distinguish between the Sanctus ("Holy, holy, holy") and the Benedictus ("Blessed is he who comes..."). Since they are most often sung together, one immediately after the other, I will consider them as a single unit.

[44] Jungmann, vol. 2, 130.

happened with the other segments of the ordinary of the mass, composers eventually created music too complicated for untrained singers, and the choir took over the congregation's role in singing the Sanctus.

The other text commonly associated with communion, the Agnus Dei, was brought into Western liturgy from the Eastern Church around the seventh century.[45] It was sung by both choir and congregation to a simple melody until, as with the Sanctus, musical complexity eradicated the people's participation.[46]

Although they were added at different times between the fourth and the eleventh centuries, these repeated texts became the ordinary of the mass: the parts that must be present even as the prayers, readings, and praises proper to each liturgical feast or fast day changed. Yet over the centuries, these prayers slowly lost their identity as a vehicle for the people's participation. Medieval and Renaissance composers created glorious and complex musical settings for these texts, and increasingly choirs, rather than the congregation, sang these words of prayer, praise, and proclamation of faith. This movement led to the majestic and lengthy masses of Mozart, Haydn, Schubert, and Beethoven, works that are now used far more frequently in the concert hall than in the sanctuary.

The Church did not entirely lose the ideal of worship anchored by core congregational song, however. This ideal lived on in two ways. First, it affected the liturgical direction that sixteenth-century reformers chose in the new movements they created, as will be seen below.

---

[45] Ibid., 333-334.

[46] Ibid., 337.

Second, the Catholic Church later regained an appreciation for the role of the congregation, especially in twentieth-century liturgical renewal. Recent composers have created musical settings of the Kyrie, Gloria, Creed, Sanctus, and Agnus Dei that allow congregations once again to sing these ancient texts as they did centuries ago.

We find many traces of the influence of the ordinary of the mass on Protestant reformations, as mentioned above. Rather than abandoning all of the worship practices of Roman Catholicism, as is sometimes assumed, Martin Luther retained much of the liturgy and music that had built up the faith of his congregation before the Reformation. As he grew bolder in his liturgical experimentation, Luther translated the mass into German. Where possible, he borrowed and tweaked the familiar melodies of the ordinary of the mass to fit the new rhythms and accents of the German text.[47] And when necessary, Luther sought new music to accompany the distinctive rhythms of his new German translations. For example, in Luther's *Deutsche Messe* he retained the Agnus Dei, which could be sung using one of two different German translations: "*Christe, du Lamm Gottes*," or "*O Lamm Gottes unschuldig*."[48] The Anglican Church, likewise, retained most of the ordinary of the mass in its weekly worship, simply translated into English.

The Calvinist and Zwinglian branches of the Reformation, however, engaged in a more thorough purging of Roman influence. These leaders distrusted the set forms that they believed Rome had imposed on the pattern of Christian worship, and they sought to wipe

---

[47] Andrew Wilson-Dickson, *The Story of Christian Music*, paperback ed., (Minneapolis: Fortress Press, 2003), 62.

[48] James Robert Davidson, *A Dictionary of Protestant Church Music*, (Metuchen, New Jersey: Scarecrow Press, 1975), 19.

away these accretions in order to worship more nearly as did Christ's early followers. Although Ulrich Zwingli eliminated all sung worship, thereby dismissing both text and tune of the ordinary of the mass, John Calvin believed that singing in Church was a form of prayer.[49] Yet he distrusted the texts of the ordinary of the mass, many of which are based on various scriptural texts but are not always direct biblical quotations. Calvin chose to limit his congregation to the singing of the Psalms, supplemented by a few traditional texts including the Lord's Prayer and the Nunc dimittis[50], thereby using purely biblical texts that would be beyond reproach. In this way, he created a new "ordinary," one that was as limited, and as formative, as the Kyrie, Gloria, Credo, Sanctus, and Agnus Dei were.

The liturgical and ecumenical movements of the twentieth century have encouraged more Protestant denominations to employ at least some of the elements of the ordinary of the mass. Since these texts are understood as ancient and therefore belonging to all Christians, their use has become a symbol of Christian unity beyond the bounds of both time and denomination. Although the ordinary of the mass and other repeated texts for worship still remain foreign to many congregations, a large number of Christians now participate in some way in the use of formal-liturgical music.

---

[49] Paul Westermeyer, *Te Deum: the Church and Music*, (Minneapolis: Fortress Press, 1998), 155.

[50] The Nunc dimittis, also called the Song or Canticle of Simeon, is found in Luke 2:29-32. This canticle traditionally features during the nighttime prayer ritual known as Compline. It served as a fixed form of sung prayer within the daily round of the divine office much as the Kyrie and the Sanctus serve that role in the mass.

THE CATECHETICAL FUNCTION OF FORMAL LITURGICAL TEXTS

How does music function in the formal-liturgical tradition? How is it expected to assist the congregation in worship? It will be helpful to look at the function of the texts and the music to which these texts are sung separately.

The core texts of formal-liturgical worship engage the congregation in theological formation. The use of repeated musical elements in worship, sung Sunday after Sunday, builds the congregation's understanding of itself, its faith, and its relationship to God. As Martin Luther wrote in his preface to a volume of burial hymns, God "is thereby praised and honored and we are made better and stronger in faith when his holy Word is impressed on our hearts by sweet music."[51] He describes the way in which repetition of texts, aided by attractive melodies, impresses correct theology and holy faith on malleable human hearts. Just as students repeat multiplication tables aloud in order to memorize them, the communal and audible singing of the Gloria, for example, helps us retain the images and understandings of Christ as only begotten Son, Lamb of God, and One who takes away the sins of the world.

While it is clear that music in formal-liturgical worship also serves to praise and to pray to God, a strong tendency toward faith formation, or catechesis, exists in this repertoire. Catechesis is "the process of instructing new converts to Christianity," although more recent usages of the word also imply an ongoing education that

---

[51] Luther, 328.

continues long after one has joined the Church.[52] Moreover, there are strong historic links between catechesis and liturgy. From the beginning, catechesis has connoted an oral process in which the faith is handed on to others just as it was received, with much the same fidelity with which the core texts of the mass have been handed on. Even more, the "context in which this whole teaching [catechesis] was situated was the liturgy."[53] Christians were instructed in order to participate in, and through participating in, the mass. The Nicene Creed formed part of the basis for early catechetical instruction, which included doctrinal, moral, and liturgical dimensions. Contemporary Catholic and Protestant thought confirms this connection between instruction and worship, asserting that catechesis can take place in many circumstances, including in worship.[54] As phrased in a recent statement by the Music Subcommittee of the Committee on Divine Worship of the United States Conference of Catholic Bishops, "[p]articipation [through singing] in the Sacred Liturgy both expresses and strengthens the faith that is in us."[55]

Other witnesses throughout Christian history have recognized the formative potential of music in worship. According to scholar Paul Bradshaw, this function of music and worship was critical to the desert ascetics of the early fourth century. Communities of ascetics gathered

---

[52] *The HarperCollins Dictionary of Religion*, s.v. "catechesis." See also "catechesis" in *The Oxford Dictionary of the Christian Church*, 3rd ed.

[53] *Sacramentum Mundi*, s.v. "catechesis."

[54] Ibid. For a Reformed perspective on the power of worship to mold character, see Kendra G. Hotz and Matthew T. Mathews, *Shaping the Christian Life: Worship and the Religious Affections* (Louisville: Westminster John Knox Press, 2006). E. Byron Anderson brings a Methodist perspective to the same topic in his *Worship and Christian Identity: Practicing Ourselves* (Collegeville, Minnesota: The Liturgical Press, 2003).

[55] *Sing to the Lord: Music in Divine Worship* (Washington, D.C.: United States Conference of Catholic Bishops, 2007), 5.

twice each day to listen to scripture passages, both sung and spoken, alternating with silence for meditation. For these monks and hermits, "the primary purpose of the extended meditation was formation: the monk meditated on the scriptures, and especially the psalms, in order to grow into the likeness of Christ."[56] Later Catholic teaching located the formative potential of worship particularly in the congregation's musical participation. In Chapter VI of *Sacrosanctum Concilium*, the Second Vatican Council defined the purposes of sacred music as the "[glorification] of God and the sanctification of the faithful."[57] According to this document, the singing of ancient and orthodox songs can form the congregation into a more holy Body. This principle is not new but rather continues a Catholic understanding of role of music in worship. Pope Pius X, more than sixty years before the Second Vatican Council, described the function of sacred music as "to clothe with befitting melody the liturgical text proposed for the understanding of the faithful."[58]

Liturgical scholar Gordon Lathrop describes this catechetical formation using the metaphors of geography and cosmology. He believes that "Christian liturgy [including music] orients its participants in the world."[59] The words sung in worship, as part of the entire liturgical *ordo*, give singers the ability to understand the world around

---

[56] Bradshaw, *Reconstructing*, 110.

[57] www.vatican.va/archive/hist_councils/ii_vatican_council/documents/vat-ii_const_19631204_sacrosanctum-concilium_en.html, accessed May 31, 2010.

[58] Miriam Therese Winter, *Why Sing? Toward a Theology of Catholic Church Music*, (Washington, DC, The Pastoral Press, 1984), 161.

[59] Gordon Lathrop, *Holy Ground: A Liturgical Cosmology* (Minneapolis: Fortress Press, 2003), 51.

them. Even more, Lathrop implies that this orienting function can include creating, as well as mapping, our context.

> For some Aboriginal groups, the "songs" – the rituals known by the people – are ancient gifts from the ancestors, the very ancestors who were involved in making the features of the landscape in the Dreamtime. The songs helped to make the landscape, represent the landscape, are actually etched upon the landscape, though that etching may be seen only in the ritual. In any case, to sing the songs is to sing a map through the world. Christians also believe that the word that made the world is the very word around which they assemble and, graciously, the very word put in their mouths to sing. Also for Christians, this word actually etches its lines upon the landscape. This word gives a way to walk through the world.[60]

Thus, those who sing the Creed and the Gloria, among other texts, find that these words both guide us in navigating our world and, to some extent, form the world itself.

Luther finds the source of the texts to be sung in "holy Word," or the scriptures. Likewise, congregations in the formal-liturgical tradition are careful to employ texts that either come directly from the Bible, such as the Psalms of the Reformed practice, or from highly trustworthy interpreters of Biblical truth. We see an example of the latter case in the Nicene Creed, formulated by the ecumenical council at Chalcedon. Other texts for worship, including the *Te Deum* and the *Phos hilaron*, arose in the early centuries of the Christian faith and survived the rigorous scrutiny of generations of Christians to earn their place in the canon of core Christian worship texts. Since anything that is repeated often enough will be remembered, leaders of the faithful have always found it

---

[60] Ibid., 54.

critical to select texts that will form a "better and stronger" faith in the congregation. The Gloria and the Creed offer lengthy explanations of who God is. The Sanctus, Agnus Dei, and Kyrie give shorter prayers of humility before the Lord. Together, these texts form the congregation into a people who pray and praise with an orthodox understanding of the God they worship and their own relationship to God.

The earliest Christian gatherings likely adopted the Jewish practice of chanting or singing sacred texts. Such singing made readings and prayers more audible in an age without electronic amplification. It also set apart these ritual forms of communication, making prayers and sacred songs sound different from, and more elevated than, quotidian speech. In time, such chanting became more ornate and evolved as secular musical practices changed. But from the beginning, prayers, psalms, scripture readings, and responses were sung as often as or even more often than they were spoken.

THE AESTHETIC AND ENCULTURATING ROLE OF FORMAL-LITURGICAL MUSIC

Given that many of the sung texts of the formal-liturgical tradition are repeated each week, the music of these texts serves the vital purpose of re-vesting the liturgy in beauty, reverence, and relevance. People of all cultures and musical traditions, from different generations and from diverse locations, have set the unchanging texts of the formal-liturgical tradition to music fitting their context. Music can make a text feel at home within a particular location, for a particular age group, or among those who prefer a certain style of music. Tune and accompaniment can also help a fixed song or prayer evolve with the changing seasons of the church year.

To fully explore this concept, let us examine the Gloria as an example. The *Liber Usualis*, a collection of ancient plainchant to be used in worship among Roman Catholics in early twentieth century, contains eighteen different melodies for the Gloria.[61] These vary from simple, syllabic settings to ornate and complex melodies. The Gloria for Feasts of the Holy Virgin, found in Example 1, lies on the complex side of this continuum, making use of a wide range and employing several melismas.[62]

Even so, it carries the communal ethos of plainchant, in which the singers attempt to create one unified prayer out of their many voices. The unity of melodic performance implies a Christian unity to which medieval monastic communities (out of which this repertoire arose) aspired. The use of Latin and unmetered music fosters an attitude of otherworldliness, hinting at a God more transcendent than imminent. These plainchant Glorias also, by virtue of being *a cappella* and monophonic, express a simplicity and austerity that adhere well to the ideals of medieval Christian monasticism.

---

[61] *Paroissien Romain,* (Tournai, Belgium: Desclée et Cie, 1931). Since this copy of the *Liber Usualis* was printed for French-speaking users, it has a slightly different name. The contents of the book, however, are identical in all copies of the *Liber.* The Gloria for Feasts of the Holy Virgin is found on pages 38-40.

[62] A melisma is one syllable that is sung to several notes. One of the most well-known melismas is found on the word "gloria" in the Christmas hymn "Angels We Have Heard on High."

Gloria for Feasts of the Holy Virgin

Example 1

The same Gloria text sounds entirely different in the early Lutheran congregations of Germany. Nicholaus Decius translated the Latin text of the Gloria into a metric German version, "Allein Gott in der Hoh sei Her," in 1525 (see Example 2).

247   All Glory Be to God on High

1 All glo - ry be to God on high, and peace on
2 O Lamb of God, Lord Je - sus Christ, whom God the
3 You on - ly are the Ho - ly One who came for

earth from heav - en, and God's good - will un - fail - ing -
Fa - ther gave us, who for the world was sac - ri -
our sal - va - tion, and on - ly you are God's true

ly be to his peo - ple giv - en. Al - might - y
ficed up - on the cross to save us, at God's right
Son who was be - fore cre - a - tion. You on - ly,

God, you are our King: we wor - ship you, our thanks we
hand you in - ter - cede for those who for your mer - cy
Christ, as Lord we own, and with the Spir - it you a -

bring, we praise you for your glo - ry.
plead; re - ceive the prayer we of - fer.
lone share in the Fa - ther's glo - ry.

Text: Latin: Gloria in excelsis Deo, 4th cent.; vers. Nikolaus Decius, 1525; tr. F. Bland Tucker, 1977, alt.
© 1985, The Church Pension Fund. Used by permission.
Tune: attr. Nikolaus Decius, 1539

87 87 887
ALLEIN GOTT

Example 2[63]

---

[63] "All Glory Be to God on High," as found in the *Psalter Hymnal* (Grand Rapids:
CRC Publications, 1987), 247. From 1982, © the Church Pension Fund.
All rights reserved. Used by permission of Church Publishing
Incorporated, New York, NY.

39

The tune to which this new translation was set is also attributed to Decius. Interestingly, the author and composer chose to adapt a small portion of the Easter plainchant melody for the Gloria in creating his new tune, a common practice among early Lutheran hymn-writers and musicians.[64] But the austerity and subtlety of the ancient chant is replaced here with a vigorous optimism, created by conforming the tune to triple meter. Decius also added melodic repetitions to his music, making the tune easier to sing and bringing it in line with the common Lutheran chorale form of the time, also known as bar form.[65] Reborn through new music and a new translation, this Gloria is exuberant, solid, and accessible: it suits the young and vigorous Lutheran church for which it was created.

In the early 1960's, before the revolutionary changes of Vatican II, the Roman Catholic Church continued to mandate worship in Latin. One inventive missionary priest, however, determined to break whatever musical barriers he could for the people he served. Borrowing heavily from the musical style and melodies of the people of the Congo, Father Guido Haazen and the musicians of his congregation created the *Missa Luba*, a composition encompassing all five parts of the common of the mass. But whereas the language of the text is in Latin, the music is purely Congolese: the call-and-response texture, the multi-layered percussion accompaniment, the periodic eruption of improvisation (impossible to notate but audible on recordings), and many other

---

[64] Emily R. Brink and Bert Polman, eds., *Psalter Hymnal Handbook*, (Grand Rapids: CRC Publications, 1998), 386.

[65] Bar form has nothing to do with pubs. Instead, it is a simple musical form in which the opening part of a melody is repeated; the second part offers contrast but often ends similarly to the first part. Musicians diagram bar form using the letters AAB.

factors make this a mass of the Congo in all aspects but language.[66] The texts of the Medieval Catholic mass have been reclothed in musical garments appropriate to the culture and spirituality of the Congo.

Composer David Haas wrote a contrasting Gloria for his 1988 *Mass of Light*, to be sung in modern Roman Catholic worship (see Example 3, which provides an excerpt of this work). This version uses an English translation of the text, sung by both cantor and congregation. The congregation is given a simple and joyful refrain, using the opening words of the Gloria from Luke's gospel, with which it periodically interrupts the cantor's line. The cantor sings the rest of the Gloria, in segments of varying length. Since the text is not metric, its words do not fit precisely in rhythmically identical phrases. This constant shifting of accent and phrase length can make texts like the Gloria difficult for congregations to sing, unless they are paraphrased metrically, as in the Decius version. However, the American Catholic Church has developed a system for being able to sing such texts with congregational participation but without taxing the congregation's musical ability. In this system, cantors and choirs sing the bulk of the text in question, bringing the congregation in with a repeatable refrain from time to time. This system is used widely for psalms, which are included at each Sunday worship service, but it works well for the Gloria, too. Other denominations have also begun to experiment with this method for singing, yet the system is most commonly found in the Catholic Church.

---

[66] The *Missa Luba* was recorded in 1958 and issued as *Les Troubadours Du Roi Baudouin – Missa Luba* in the Netherlands by Philips Records BL 7592. The Gloria from the 1965 US release of the recording is available for listening on-line at: https://www.youtube.com/watch?v=G4jeTWheAxA

2276   Glory to God in the Highest

WORDS: From the liturgy (Luke 2:14; John 1:29; Eph. 1:20-21)
MUSIC: David Haas (from *Mass of Light*)
© 1988 GIA Publications, Inc.

GLORIA (HAAS)
Irregular with Refrain

Example 3[67]

---

[67] Example 3 is found in *The Faith We Sing*, singer's edition, (Nashville: Abingdon Press, 2000), 2276. © 1988, GIA Publications, Inc. Used by permission.

These four examples hint at the endless variety with which music can re-vest the repeated texts of the formal-liturgical tradition. In each case, the text continues to impart the tenets of the Christian faith, but the music aligns that faith with beauty as seen through the eyes of the people of different times and cultures. Certainly, one can also find examples of the Gloria, or other texts from the core repertoires of Christian worship, set to music for professional musicians rather than the congregation. Yet as we are attending to the function of congregational singing in this study, we may pass over the ways in which those more complicated musical settings express the text in ways appropriate to their time and place.

SCRIPTURAL INSTANCES OF THE CATECHETICAL ROLE OF MUSIC

Christians often, and rightly, turn to the Bible when seeking to understand new ideas or ancient problems. While the scriptures cannot predict the details and questions of twenty-first century life, they do ground us in the history of God's chosen people, God's incarnate entry into human life, and God's promises of salvation. When exploring ways of using music in worship, we may look to the Bible for examples of these usages, warnings about possible abuses, or glimpses of theological insight. So let us begin by looking for instances of music serving a catechetical role in worship.

We frequently find the command to recite God's great deeds in the scriptures. The psalm of thanksgiving found in 1 Chronicles 16, following immediately after the description of David appointing Asaph and his family to be liturgical musicians, commands "O give thanks to the Lord, call on his name, make known his deeds among the peoples. Sing to him, sing praises to him, tell of all his wonderful works." Twice, the followers of God are told that their singing and praise must include the recitation or repetition of God's saving acts. Psalm 89 extends this call, demonstrating a retelling that reaches beyond the current congregation: "I will sing of your steadfast love, O Lord, forever; with my mouth I will proclaim your faithfulness to all generations" (vs. 1). Similar passages are found in Psalms 101:1, 119:172, and 138:5. These verses suggest that the praise of God should often, if not always, be rooted in what we know of the character and actions of God. Including the retelling of these things strengthens our understanding of who God is, and why, therefore, we have good reason to praise. Clearly, such a retelling serves an evangelistic purpose, and may summon others to the worship of God. Yet it also grounds the singer's own worship in a growing knowledge of who God is and what God has done. Within the ordinary of the mass, the Gloria and the Credo, in particular, seem to continue this practice for congregations that sing these texts.

Several psalms, particularly ones that belong in part or whole to the category of wisdom literature, also refer explicitly to teaching.[68] In Psalm 32, the psalmist declares "I will instruct you and teach you the way you should go; I will counsel you with my eye upon you" (NRSV). Such an instructional section is included and expanded upon in Psalm 34, and present briefly in Psalm 51. In other psalms, the singer seeks wisdom him- or herself, asking God to "teach me" the way, right paths, wisdom, God's statutes, good judgment, and to do God's will (see Psalms 25, 27, 51, 86, 119, and 143). It must be noted, however, that there is

---

[68] Many psalms contain admonitions to learn about God or obey God's teachings. Psalms that lean in this direction may be considered wisdom psalms. Psalms 1, 34, 37, 39, 49, 73, 90, 111, 112, 119, and 145 are examples of psalms with a wisdom approach or emphasis. Other wisdom literature in the Bible includes the books of Proverbs, Ecclesiastes, and Job. See Erhard S. Gerstenberger, *Psalms Part I, with an Introduction to Cultic Poetry,* The Forms of Old Testament Literature, eds. Rolf Knierim and Gene M. Tucker, no. 14 (Grand Rapids, MI: Eerdmans, 1988), 19-20.

not universal agreement that these psalms would have been used, much less sung, in the context of worship. Many scholars of the psalms have argued instead that wisdom psalms were used in private devotional or educational contexts. These scholars point to such details as acrostic structure, sophisticated literary style, and theological rather than doxological orientation to prove their point. Speaking for the opposite point of view, Erhard Gerstenberger believes that

> all these so-called wisdom psalms in reality were liturgical pieces from the very beginning. Their changed appearance and their different message are due solely to the changed conditions of worship during and after the Exile... These early [exiled] Jewish communities fought against religious extermination, insisting on the one, exclusive, and invisible God, on his *tora*, on his Sabbath, and on his stipulations concerning food, marriage, and all the other matters of daily life... To maintain such a dynamic tradition the Jews studied the written heritage of their ancestors. Teaching this revealed will of God became the very backbone of communal and individual existence. At this point wisdom influence entered Jewish life and, most of all, Jewish cult.[69]

Given the division of opinion on this topic, one should not assume that the presence of wisdom literature in the psalms necessarily implies that such a didactic approach was present in Jewish worship. Yet this remains a possible interpretation.

Regarding the music fitting for such retelling, musicians of the formal-liturgical traditions might point to Psalm 29, attributed to David, where the psalmist instructs "Ascribe to the Lord the glory of his name; worship the Lord in holy splendor." Much has been made of this last phrase as it appears in an earlier translation: "in the beauty of holiness." Since God has done such marvelous deeds as are recounted in worship, God is worthy of glory and holy splendor. The only music fitting for the

---

[69] Ibid.

45

worship of such a God, in this way of thinking, is beautiful, splendorous music.

Harold Best offers a wise caution regarding this verse. He calls his readers to remain alert for times when we reverse the phrase, and act as if we believe that beauty causes holiness, rather than merely reflects it.[70] However, many musicians continue to strive for reverent beauty in their work at church, believing that musical beauty conveys a sense of the true splendor of God's being and character as well as the holiness to which all Christians aspire. Of course, cultural understandings of beauty change frequently. Within the formal-liturgical tradition, this constant reevaluation of what is beautiful requires the continual composition of new musical vessels for the unchanging words chosen to reflect on all that God has done.

CRITICISM OF THE CATECHETICAL USE OF MUSIC IN THE FORMAL-LITURGICAL TRADITION

All styles of worship and music are subject to criticism, from within each style as well as from without. Especially during times of musical and liturgical turmoil, when advocates of one style may be quick to critique other styles, it is helpful to look clearly and analytically at the possible shortcomings as well as the strengths of each of the musical traditions we will explore.

First, the sheer repetition that makes up a great part of formal-liturgical musical practice can draw criticism. Many feel that using the same words over and over, Sunday after Sunday, can render the

---

[70] Harold Best, *Music Through the Eyes of Faith*, (San Francisco: Harper, 1993), 148.

congregation insensitive to their meaning. Rote memorization can sometimes lead to taking songs, prayers, and texts for granted: to offering words with the mouth that do not resonate in the heart. Yet the deep familiarity that comes with memorization can also be a source of comfort at times when unexpected circumstances shake all else away. At those times, the words of the Credo or the Kyrie may become the "sighs too deep for words," that help us pray when we cannot summon up our own words.

Timothy Quill speaks to this critique when he writes:

> It has been said that the Liturgy is boring. It is like water flowing over a waterfall and boring into a rock. Eventually the water has its way with the seemingly impenetrable rock. Repetition ingrains the Word of God deep into our minds and hearts. Thus, the Word of God is there in times of crisis, persecution, sudden tragedy, and old age to comfort us with what is familiar and sure. Times of tragedy and trial do not require novelty.[71]

One would be wise to bear in mind both the numbing tendency of repetition as well as its ability to ingrain truth into our hearts and minds.

A second, related critique often raised concerning music in formal-liturgical worship is that of its overly calcified structure. With so many of its texts and musical settings fixed, formal-liturgical worship can seem to leave little room for the Holy Spirit to breathe, trouble, or convict us, or for pastors or musicians to change plans, texts, or songs when something new becomes a focus. As Don Williams, a participant in the Jesus Movement and a Presbyterian pastor, phrases the problem, "liturgical worship eliminates the free expression and the sharing of the

---

[71] Quill, 37.

Spirit's gifts that are so much at the heart of the New Testament."[72] Certainly the Spirit is as capable of moving during a worship planning session as during a worship service, and therefore a service of worship may be "Spirit-led" even if it is pre-planned to the tiniest detail. Yet Williams accurately points out that most formal-liturgical worship leaves little room for congregation members to share unexpected gifts. Musically, this means that while all are encouraged to participate in singing the psalms, prayers, hymns, or service music, rarely are different songs solicited, or new songs created, on the spot.

Modern critics, in particular, often observe that formal-liturgical worship seems to engage the head far more than it does the heart. Joe Horness describes the situation thus: "worship cannot be just about receiving great truth or theology, however profound that truth is... Worship is the response we offer to what we have received... It is one thing for my children to receive a gift at Christmas. It is quite another when they jump around and cheer and throw their arms around me with heartfelt thanks."[73] The music of the formal-liturgical traditions usually attempts to mirror the transcendent and all-powerful God who is worshipped rather than enliven and encourage congregational emotions and gratitude. This critique points at different assumptions of what the purpose of worship music should be, a constant source of misunderstanding for all who participate in the Church. But it also offers a valid concern: if we are called as whole people to worship, with mind and heart and body equally engaged, then the music of the formal-

---

[72] Don Williams, "A Charismatic Worship Response to Formal-Liturgical Worship," in *Exploring the Worship Spectrum*, ed. Paul Basden, (Grand Rapids: Zondervan, 2004), 46.

[73] Joe Horness, "A Contemporary Worship Response to Formal-Liturgical Worship," in *Exploring the Worship Spectrum*, ed. Paul Basden, (Grand Rapids: Zondervan, 2004), 42.

liturgical style must offer places for the heart and the body to enter into the worship experience, too.

INTRODUCING THIS FUNCTION INTO THE WORSHIP OF OTHER TRADITIONS

Is there something in the formal-liturgical approach to church music from which those in other worship traditions might draw? Anyone seeking to create more opportunities for formation in Christian doctrine and faith might find parts of this approach helpful. Indeed, the weekly worship of a community contributes to the formation of beliefs, habits, and character among members of the congregation, whether this is intended by worship leaders or not. It seems prudent to understand and utilize this function of worship intentionally. Yet paying attention to the catechetical nature of singing in worship need not mandate the drastic addition of the complete ordinary of the mass. Pastoral sensitivity suggests that smaller steps would make for an easier beginning for congregations unused to singing repeated texts each week in worship. Below are some strategies for incorporating part of the formal-liturgical function of music in small ways.

It is often easiest to begin with what is already familiar. If there is a prayer that the congregation uses each week, that prayer could be sung instead of spoken. Most congregations are quite familiar with the Lord's Prayer, even if they don't use it weekly. In addition, most Christians would agree that the Lord's Prayer should be formative to their faith, as Jesus taught his disciples to pray using that text.[74] This

---

[74] See Matthew 6:9-13 and Luke 11:2-4. While neither of these texts include the final doxology ("for thine is the kingdom, and the power, and the glory, for ever and ever. Amen"), the practice of adding a similar phrase to the Biblical texts appeared within the first few centuries of the Church.

may be a simple place to begin incorporating a catechetical aspect to the congregation's musical practices. There are countless musical versions of the Lord's Prayer, allowing a congregation to reframe the familiar words with fresh musical settings from time to time. An easy place to start might be the Jim Strathdee 1977 version, which works entirely as a call-and-response piece. The leader sings out each phrase, which the congregation then sings in turn. Since each phrase is repeated exactly as the leader sings it, the congregation can sing this Lord's Prayer without a hymnal or musical score, simply by listening and repeating. Although the aesthetic sensibility of this music is more folk-oriented than much of the formal-liturgical canon, its accessibility makes it a great place to start. Once the congregation is comfortable singing this prayer, it could learn other versions, appropriate for various seasons or occasions.

Certain sections of the ordinary of the mass particularly lend themselves to being sung. The Gloria, for example is the song of the angels at Christ's birth, a statement of praise so joyful that it begs to be sung rather than spoken. Likewise, the Sanctus is the song of the seraphim in Isaiah's vision and the branch-waving crowds as Jesus rode into Jerusalem. It, like the Gloria, is exuberant and quickly repays congregations that learn to sing it. Both Sanctus and Gloria can be found in numerous musical settings appropriate for congregational singing. If the congregation becomes accustomed to singing a familiar text such as the Lord's Prayer, the Gloria and Sanctus can serve as the next step for a church interested in singing catechetically.

Another approach to incorporating a formal-liturgical practice of music in the congregation might start with the question of formation.

Currently, most Protestants use this phrase and the Orthodox Church includes a similar doxology, but most Catholics recite the prayer without this final phrase.

In what way do the pastor and minister of music discern that the congregation could strengthen its spiritual and doctrinal formation? Reformed congregations adopting the Belhar Confession[75] and striving to encourage equality and solidarity with other Christians might set that text, or a portion of it, to music. United Methodist congregations wanting to incorporate the recent Companion Litany to the Social Creed[76] might wish to sing rather than speak that text. Any Christian congregation could find a musical setting of the Apostles' or Nicene Creed to employ in its worship. Each of these would reinforce educational work being done in Sunday School classes or small group discussions, demonstrating the connection between our understanding of and our worship of God.

The formal-liturgical use of music in worship encourages the congregation to root itself deeply in texts that form theological understandings and link Christians to those of previous ages. These texts are clothed in music that reflects God's glory and supreme worth. Yet these functions for text and tune are not the only ways of understanding what music in worship should do. The next chapter will

---

[75] The Belhar Confession arose out of the Dutch Reformed church in South Africa, which found apartheid antithetical to the Christian gospel. After being written in the 1980's and used locally in South Africa, Belhar's emphasis on justice, unity, and reconciliation commended it to other Reformed communities. In 2010, the Reformed Church in America ratified adoption of this confession, which is available at: www.rca.org/sslpage.aspx?pid=304 (accessed September 7, 2011).

[76] The Companion Litany to the Social Creed arose as a more poetic alternative to the United Methodist Social Creed, which dates to 1972. This new text was named a "Companion Litany," rather than a replacement to the old creed, in 2008. Both texts can be found at: www.umc-gbcs.org/site/c.frLJK2PKLqF/b.3713143/k.2AF8/182166_VII_Our_Soc ial_Creed/apps/nl/newsletter.asp (accessed September 7, 2011). The Companion Litany has already been set to music and sung in worship.

investigate traditions in which music is used to foster unified congregational response.

Chapter 3: Singing in the Hymn Tradition
Song as Congregational Response

Much of [the church's musical] heritage is exegetical or proclamatory: music helps to proclaim, to interpret, to break open the word of God. That is in part what happens when the congregation sings.[77]

... music is the taut rope that pulls us through every possible situation... It's not only a rope given by God, it's a rope we make strong with our faith, our voices, the contributions we throw into things – our words, our efforts, our music... When we sing, we all use our bodies. We all lift our lungs; we breathe in and out together; we keep the pitch together. What I am doing with my body connects me with other bodies – even bodies of the past. We sustain the spirits of the past through this physical act of singing.[78]

What is a hymn? The term is used so often for such a variety of musical material that it is worth deciding on a definition before continuing further. First of all, the term hymn refers to a poetic text, not to the music to which these texts are usually sung. Properly, the music for a hymn is called a hymn tune. Secondly, a hymn text is commonly written in strophic form, containing a number of stanzas that follow a fixed, regular pattern of syllables.[79] As we will see later, the use of

---

[77] Paul Westermeyer, *The Church Musician*, rev. ed. (Minneapolis: Augsburg Fortress, 1997), 34.

[78] Jean Janzen, quoted in Marlene Kropf and Kenneth Nafziger, *Singing: A Mennonite Voice* (Scottdale, Pennsylvania: Herald Press, 2001), 49-50.

[79] On the reasons why the term "stanza" is more appropriate than the commonly used "verse," see Harry Eskew and Hugh T. McElrath, *Sing with Understanding: an Introduction to Christian Hymnology* (Nashville: Church Street Press, 1995), 14.

alternate forms, including poetic forms with a repeated refrain following each stanza, has served as grounds for excluding particular texts from the corpus of hymnody. Thirdly, hymns are written to be sung by congregations. Authors write texts that must fit comfortably in the hearts and mouths of average people in ordinary congregations. The tunes for these hymns must also be appropriate for unrehearsed amateur performance, such as happens on Sunday mornings. Finally, Christian hymns must relate in some way to the interaction between God and humanity that occurs in worship. Hymns of praise or confession or prayer may be sung directly to God. Scriptural hymns or statements of faith may be sung to put the congregation's "Amen" on the faith that has been expressed in Bible reading and sermon. Hymns of encouragement may be addressed by the congregation to its own members, fostering each one's devotion and relationship with God. Although these texts do not of necessity always address God in the second person, they must refer in some way to the relationship between God's people and their Creator.

THE HISTORY OF HYMN SINGING

Christians have been singing hymns from the very beginning of the faith. Jesus himself sang with his disciples at the end of their Passover celebration, just one day before his crucifixion. Paul recommended the singing of "psalms, hymns, and spiritual songs" to the Christian communities at Ephesus and Galatia, although he neglected to distinguish among these three rather indeterminate categories. As the Church grew, Christians wrote hymns that became tied to the practice of the daily office: interrupting the day at fixed times for prayer, psalmody, and the singing of an appropriate hymn. The office hours of Matins (an early morning vigil), Lauds (morning prayer), Vespers (evening prayer) and Compline (bedtime prayer), as well as the briefer "little hours" of

Prime, Terce, Sext, and None (which punctuated the day at the first, third, sixth, and ninth hours) each included hymns specific to the time of day at which the worship occurred. Hymns for the service of Terce at mid-morning, for example, might mention the coming of the Holy Spirit upon the disciples at Pentecost, said to have happened at nine o'clock in the morning.[80] While not always present in the Mass, hymns flourished in Christian worship in the West.[81]

Many of the Protestant reformers also adopted hymnody as a vehicle for congregational song. Martin Luther fostered the writing and singing of chorales, sung hymn texts derived from the ordinary of the mass, from loose scripture paraphrases, or newly created. These hymns were set to sturdy tunes appropriate for congregational singing, and the chorale became the musical heritage of the Lutheran Church for centuries. The Anabaptists, also known as Swiss Brethren, began a compilation of original hymn texts that was first published in 1564 as the *Ausbund*, a collection still in use among the Amish.

The English-speaking world, however, shunned hymnody for centuries in favor of Anglican service music (similar to that described in the previous chapter) and metrical psalmody, heavily influenced by the Reformed communities of continental Europe. The psalms were theologically attractive since they derived from scriptural texts; they

---

[80] For more examples of hymns from specific hours of prayer within the daily office, see Erik Routley, *A Panorama of Christian Hymnody*, ed. Paul A. Richardson (Chicago: GIA Publications, 2005), 123-128.

[81] Beginning in the tenth century, the sequence was added to the Mass immediately following the Alleluia, which the sequence interpreted or extended. As sequences were metrical and commonly rhymed, they were a form of hymn. In the sixteenth century, Catholic liturgical reforms eliminated all but four of these sequences from use. John Harper, *The Forms and Orders of Western Liturgy from the Tenth to the Eighteenth Century* (New York: Clarendon Press, 1991), 117-118.

were practical for congregations since the short melodies to which they were set were easy to learn and repeated with each stanza. The intense and long-lived popularity of psalm singing among English congregations tentatively made room for hymns of human composure in the late 1600's. Yet the full force of English hymns exploded only in the 1700's, ushered in by Isaac Watts and Charles Wesley.

Watts, who published his first collection of hymns in 1705, created a hymnic reformation with his corpus of hundreds of new and eventually widely-accepted texts. Watts' hymns were set in simple meters and filled with a Reformed emphasis on the sovereignty of God and the dependence of sinful humanity on Christ's sacrifice.[82] These hymns include "Alas, and Did My Savior Bleed," "I Sing the Almighty Power of God," and "When I Survey the Wondrous Cross." In addition to authoring hymn texts, Watts also turned his attention to making new metrical versions of the psalms. In this pursuit, Watts determined to "accommodate the Book of Psalms to Christian Worship...to divest David and Asaph &c. of every other Character but that of a Psalmist and a Saint, and to make them always speak the common Sense and Language of a Christian."[83] Many of Watts' psalm translations are hardly recognizable as such, including "Jesus Shall Reign" (Psalm 72) and "Joy to the World," (Psalm 98).

Charles Wesley, on the other hand, employed an astonishing variety of poetic meters to convey the passionate depths of his Christian experience of grace.[84] His well-known hymn texts include "And Can it

---

[82] Eskew and McElrath, 135-136.

[83] Isaac Watts, Preface to *The Psalms of David Imitated in the Language of the New Testament*, in *Hymnology: A Collection of Source Readings*, ed. David Music (Lanham, Maryland: Scarecrow Press, 1996), 128.

[84] Eskew and McElrath, 138-139.

Be that I Should Gain," "Christ the Lord is Risen Today," "Jesus, Lover of My Soul," and "Hark! The Herald Angels sing." Although Wesley did not, like Watts, systematically work through the Psalter to make metrical versions of that portion of scripture, his hymns are informed by and filled with allusions to and quotations from books throughout the Bible.

Despite the great popularity of Watts' and Wesley's hymns throughout England, each of these authors was viewed with mixed emotions by leadership within the Church of England. Watts was a Dissenter, or Congregationalist, and Wesley was a part of the Methodist movement, which slowly and inevitably broke away from the Anglican Church despite Charles Wesley's love of and faithfulness to that body. Mainstream Anglicans feared "a potential threat to Anglican theological integrity" in the hymns of the Congregationalists, while they avoided the Wesleyan hymns which "were deemed to be colored by enthusiasm," a dangerous, if not exactly heretical, quality.[85] Slowly and amidst great disagreement, newly-composed hymns began to find their place among metrical psalms as an option for congregational singing throughout the latter half of the eighteenth century.

Yet hymn-writing arose as well, eventually, within the Anglican spirit of the state church. In the nineteenth century, the Church of England itself birthed a huge new addition to the canon of English-language hymns. Suspicious of the enthusiasm and doctrinal irregularities of the evangelical hymn writers, members of the Oxford and Cambridge movements turned for inspiration to the hymns of the early church, sung as part of the hours of the daily office.[86] These

---

[85] Thomas K. McCart, *The Matter and Manner of Praise: The Controversial Evolution of Hymnody in the Church of England 1760-1820* (Lanham, Md: Scarecrow Press, 1998), 35.

[86] See page 2 of this chapter.

ancient Latin and Greek texts were elegant statements of doctrinal purity, conforming to the various seasons of the Church year as well as particular times of day. John Mason Neale, among others, translated hundreds of these to produce a panoply of hymns, including "Of the Father's Love Bogotten," "Good Christian Men, Rejoice," "All Glory, Laud, and Honor," and "Come, Ye Faithful, Raise the Strain."

This was also the age when the enormous corpus of German Lutheran chorales was opened to English-speaking Christians, primarily through the translations of Catherine Winkworth. She made available such hymnic treasures as *Nun Danket Alle Gott* ("Now Thank We All Our God"), *Lobe Den Herren* ("Praise to the Lord, the Almighty"), *Wie Schon Leuchtet Der Morgenstern* ("O Morning Star, How Fair and Bright"), and *Liebster Jesu* ("Blessed Jesus, at Thy Word").

More recently, the "New English Renaissance," also called the "Hymn Explosion," has contributed a variety of new hymns to congregational repertoire.[87] These hymns bring contemporary language and modern sensibilities about theology, culture, and gender to the task of writing words to be sung in worship. Some of the leaders in this new wave of hymn writing include Fred Pratt Green ("When in our Music God is Glorified," "God is Here"), Fred Kaan ("Help Us Accept Each Other," "We Meet You, O Christ,"), and Brian Wren ("I Come with Joy," "Christ is Alive! Let Christians Sing").

Throughout this history, the term "hymn" has been used to delineate, and therefore also to exclude, certain songs of the faithful. Hymnal editors, scholars, congregations, and church leaders have, at times, been unwilling to allow certain genres into their repertoire. One

---

[87] See Eskew and McElrath, 168, and William S. Smith, *Joyful Noise* (Franklin, Tennessee: Providence House Publishers, 2007), 115.

of the most notorious of these instances involves the popular gospel songs of the nineteenth century. The term gospel was used to describe both African-American music of faith descended from spirituals as well as the simple revivalist songs popular at 1800's camp meetings and Sunday Schools.[88] Both types of gospel song were generally excluded from hymnals and American congregational worship: the former for their association with African-Americans, and the latter out of a classist assumption that the verse/chorus form and simple messages of salvation were not appropriate for true, dignified worship.

Other categories of worship music seem to lie outside of the hymn "umbrella" as well. The short, repetitive songs of the Taizé tradition are not strophic and are generally called chants or prayers. Many musical traditions from various Christian communities around the world make use of a cyclic or repeated structure rather than a traditional hymn structure of multiple stanzas; these pieces are usually referred to as global songs rather than hymns.[89] Finally, much of Contemporary Christian Music (CCM) is modeled on the stanza, bridge, and chorus structure of pop or rock songs rather than the strophic form of hymnody. These pieces of music are almost always labeled songs. A few authors, however, write contemporary lyrics that seem to fit comfortably in the hymn category. Stuart Townend, author of "In Christ

---

[88] These two genres were sometimes distinguished as "black gospel" and "white gospel." The former are marked by a marriage of African-American secular musical styles, including blues, jazz, and ragtime, to religious content. The latter include simple words, messages, tunes, and harmonies; optimistic texts about salvation paired with cheerful major keys; and choruses that could be remembered and sung by all, without regard to literacy or hymnal ownership.

[89] See especially C. Michael Hawn, *Gather into One: Praying and Singing Globally* (Grand Rapids, Michigan: Eerdmans, 2003), 224-240. Hawn writes with depth and liturgical insight about the natures of and uses for cyclic musical forms and the "sequential" form of traditional Western European Christian hymns.

Alone" and "How Deep the Father's Love," seems to favor such a strophic form when writing some of his texts.[90]

The Responsory Function of Hymns

Although hymns can be used in many places in worship, hymn texts almost always function as vehicles for congregational response. When singing a hymn, the congregation offers its thoughts, feelings, and desires to complement what has been heard in scripture, sermon, and prayer. Especially in worship that emphasizes the aural over the visual and the role of the leader over that of the congregation, hymns provide an opportunity for active and thoughtful congregational participation. Hymn texts have been written to respond to the many activities included in worship, including prayer, praise, collecting an offering, and celebrating the sacraments. But the one worship activity that seems to have elicited more hymn writing than any other is the reading of scripture. Authors and poets have taken up the challenge of writing texts that respond to hundreds of scriptural pericopes, allowing congregations to bring their own faith and their understanding of these Biblical passages into conversation with the writings of the scriptural authors. Some poets, like Watts, have attempted to bring the Biblical stories into modern language so they can be more easily understood. Others might use a portion of scripture as a springboard to explore a contemporary issue. Hymn writers have employed many approaches in crafting their sung responses to scripture.

---

[90] An interesting commentary on the writing of "How Deep the Father's Love" can be found at www.stuarttownend.co.uk/songs/storybehindthesongs/howdeepthefatherslove

HYMNS AS MIDRASHIM: SINGING OUR RESPONSE TO SCRIPTURE

Thomas Troeger names this function of hymns in a vivid way when he calls hymns "midrashim." Midrash is a form of biblical commentary from the Jewish tradition. Rabbinic scholars composed midrashim to explore and explain holy scriptures, offering varied interpretations and added details in their efforts to plumb the depths of each verse from the Torah. According to Troeger, "midrash is, then, a concept rooted in the history of biblical interpretation that allows for multiple readings of scripture in light of contemporary life. That sounds remarkably like the function of hymnody as it has flowed into new times and places and branched into many different streams."[91] Troeger finds that hymns, as they fulfill this role, are vital to the congregation's understanding of its faith. "Hymns as midrashim perform a crucial theological task: they help to save the church from bibliolatry, the turning of scripture into an idol. We do not worship the Bible... Hymns as midrashim keep the gathered church mindful that what matters is not simply the literal page but the encounter with the living God, who, like the wise rabbis, allows multiple and even conflicting interpretations of the same biblical passage."[92] We will explore this function of hymns further, looking at examples of hymn texts that respond to scripture as well as those that respond to other elements in worship.

The first of our examples draws on a passage from the first book of the Bible. In Genesis 32:22-32, we read the familiar account of Jacob wrestling with a strange man, who he later determines must be God. The scene is a brief but confusing one: Jacob is alone, having sent

---

[91] Thomas H. Troeger, *Wonder Reborn: Creating Sermons on Hymns, Music, and Poetry* (New York: Oxford University Press, 2010), 32.

[92] Ibid., 33-34.

his family ahead of him in hopes of appeasing his justifiably angry brother, Esau. The Biblical text does not clarify Jacob's feelings, his reasons for engaging in an impromptu bout with a stranger, or how it was that the mortal Jacob could prevail over his heavenly opponent. As familiar as the text is, it is a difficult one for us to fully fathom.

In 1742, Charles Wesley published a 14-stanza hymn called "Wrestling Jacob," a text that Watts found worth all of the lines of poetry he himself had ever written.[93]

> Come, O thou Traveler unknown,
> Whom still I hold but cannot see!
> My company before is gone,
> And I am left alone with thee;
> With thee all night I mean to stay
> And wrestle till the break of day.
>
> I need not tell thee who I am,
> My misery and sin declare;
> Thyself hast called me by my name,
> Look on thy hands and read it there.
> But who, I ask thee, who art thou?
> Tell me thy name and tell me now.
>
> In vain thou strugglest to get free,
> I never will unloose my hold;
> Art thou the man that died for me?
> The secret of thy love unfold;
> Wrestling, I will not let thee go
> Till I thy name, thy nature know
>
> Wilt thou not yet to me reveal
> Thy new, unutterable name?
> Tell me, I still beseech thee, tell,
> To know it now resolved I am;
> Wrestling, I will not let thee go,
> Till I thy name, thy nature know.

---

[93] Carlton R. Young, *Companion to the United Methodist Hymnal* (Nashville: Abingdon Press, 1993), 295.

What though my shrinking flesh complain
And murmur to contend so long?
I rise superior to my pain:
When I am weak then I am strong,
And when my all of strength shall fail
I shall with the God-man prevail.

My strength is gone, my nature dies,
I sink beneath thy weighty hand,
Faint to revive, and fall to rise;
I fall, and yet by faith I stand;
I stand, and will not let thee go
Till I thy name, thy nature know.

Yield to me now – for I am weak
But confident in self-despair!
Speak to my heart, in blessing speak,
Be conquered by my instant prayer:
Speak, or thou never hence shall move,
And tell me if thy name is Love.

'Tis Love! 'tis Love! Thou diedst for me,
I hear thy whisper in my heart.
The morning breaks, the shadows flee,
Pure Universal Love thou art:
To me, to all, thy mercies move –
Thy nature and thy name is Love.

My prayer hath power with God; the grace
Unspeakable I now receive;
Through faith I see thee face to face,
I see thee face to face, and live!
In vain I have not wept and strove –
Thy nature and thy name is Love.

I know thee, Savior, who thou art,
Jesus, the feeble sinner's friend;
Nor wilt thou with the night depart,
But stay and love me to the end:
Thy mercies never shall remove,
Thy nature and thy name is Love.

The Sun of Righteousness on me
Hath risen with healing in its wings:
Withered my nature's strength; from thee
My soul its life and succor brings;

My help is all laid up above;
Thy nature, and thy name is Love.

Contented now upon my thigh
I halt, till life's short journey end;
All helplessness, all weakness I
On thee alone for strength depend;
Nor have I power from thee to move:
Thy nature, and thy name is Love.

Lame as I am, I take the prey,
Hell, earth, and sin with ease overcome;
I leap for joy, pursue my way,
And as a bounding hart fly home,
Through all eternity to prove
Thy nature, and thy name is Love.

Wesley's text allows the reader to enter the biblical narrative as Jacob, "weak, but confident in self-despair." He interprets the scriptural wrestling match as a fight between the misery of human sin and the unstoppable mercy of God. Wesley makes one alteration to the story, however. Whereas in the Genesis account Jacob never learns the name of his opponent, in the hymn text he discovers that his wrestling partner is Love, who "diedst for me… pure Universal Love." Wesley's profound hymn helps the congregation enter into this odd Biblical passage, making it accessible and a witness to the power of Christ in the lives of the congregation members. All people of faith have encountered days when they feel that their "misery and sin declare" who they are before they open their mouths. And all have likewise wondered at the incomprehensible, sacrificial love of God for sinful humanity. Like Jacob in the hymn text, people of faith can try to wrestle out "the secret of [God's] love" for us. Like Jacob, they find that their infirmities help them to trust God more: "all helplessness, all weakness I on thee alone for strength depend." In singing "Wrestling Jacob," the members of the congregation can affirm and respond to Jacob's experience with their own, Christian, understanding of the text.

Another example of a hymn that responds to scripture in a midrashic fashion can be found among Isaac Watts' *Hymns and Spiritual Songs*, published in 1707. Watts dedicated the third part of that volume to hymn texts reflecting on the Lord's Supper. The first hymn in that section, therefore, responds both to the institution narrative as found in 1 Corinthians 11:23 and to the congregation's practice of communing in worship.[94]

'Twas on that dark, that doleful night
when powers of earth and hell arose
against the Son of God's delight,
and friends betrayed him to his foes:

Before the mournful scene began,
He took the bread, and blessed, and brake:
What love through all his actions ran!
What wondrous words of grace he spake!

"This is my body, broke for sin;
receive and eat the living food:"
Then took the cup, and blessed the wine;
"Tis the new cov'nant in my blood."

[For us his flesh with nails was torn,
He bore the scourge, he felt the thorn;
And justice poured upon his head
Its heavy vengeance in our stead.

For us the vital blood was spilt,
To buy the pardon of our guilt,
When, for black crimes of biggest size,
He gave his soul a sacrifice.]

"Do this, " he cried, "till time shall end,
in memory of your dying Friend;
meet at my table, and record
the love of your departed Lord."

---

[94] www.hymnary.org/text/twas_on_that_dark_that_doleful_night accessed September 27, 2012

[Jesus, thy feast we celebrate,
We show thy death, we sing thy name,
Till thou return, and we shall eat
The marriage supper of the Lamb.]

Watts responds by embroidering the scriptural passage, adding evocative details such as atmospheric descriptions (a dark, doleful, and mournful evening) and indicators of emotion (Christ cries out, rather than simply speaks, his instructions to the disciples). Additionally, the poet provides interpretation in his midrash, explaining significance and reasons that are not made explicit in Paul's letter to the Corinthians. In this vein, Watts points out the love and grace that enliven Christ's words and actions at this "mournful scene," and he explains that the whole passion, of which this meal is a part, was "to buy the pardon of our guilt." Lastly, Watts gives the congregation a chance to respond, in first person plural, to the Lord's Supper in the final stanza of the hymn. Here, the congregants can offer their celebration of the sacrament to Jesus directly, thus responding to the Corinthians text with their own words and actions.

Hymnals are full of hymns that, like "Wrestling Jacob" and "'Twas on that Dark, that Doleful Night," help the congregation to engage with biblical texts. When, awaiting the joyful celebration of Christmas, a congregation sings "Come, thou Long-Expected Jesus," people of faith respond to the Advent readings from the prophets with their own, modern-day plea for Christ to come, save, and rule. At Christmas, the people may pray "be born in us today," as they sing "O Little Town of Bethlehem," seeing the setting of Luke's Christmas story as a metaphor for their own hearts and placing themselves with the witnesses of Christ's long-ago birth. Following a reading of the first few verses in the second chapter of 2 Timothy, the congregation might reply by asking itself, "Am I a soldier of the cross, a follower of the Lamb?" using the words of Isaac Watts' timeless hymn. In the spring of 1968, Martin Luther King, Jr. was assassinated ten days before Easter. Fearing that existing Easter hymns could not help his congregation respond in gratitude and joy to the Gospel account of the resurrection while still honestly admitting their grief over the death of such an important Christian leader, minister and poet Brian Wren composed the text "Christ is Alive, Let Christians Sing!" In singing this text, his congregation could freely reply to the dual circumstances of Easter and tragedy by proclaiming:

> Not throned afar, remotely high
> untouched, unmoved by human pains,
> but daily, in the midst of life
> our Savior in the Godhead reigns.
>
> In every insult, rift, and war,
> where color, scorn, or wealth divide,
> he suffers still, yet loves the more,
> and lives, though ever crucified.[95]

SINGING OUR RESPONSE TO WORSHIP

Other clues to how hymns function can be found in the usual placement of hymns in worship. The Presbyterian *Book of Common Worship*, the Christian Reformed Church's 1987 *Psalter Hymnal*, *The United Methodist Hymnal*, *Evangelical Lutheran Worship*, the Reformed Church in America's hymnal *Rejoice in the Lord*, and the Episcopal *Book of Common Prayer* all offer recommended worship patterns, or orders,

---

[95] Verses 3 and 4 of "Christ is Alive," by Brian Wren, ©1975 Hope Publishing Company, Carol Stream, IL 60188, as found in the United Methodist Hymnal (Nashville: The United Methodist Publishing House, 1989), 318. Used by permission.

for their respective denominations. Four of these six recommend using a hymn immediately following the sermon, and two of the hymnals explicitly call this a "response" to the Word that has been shared.

Congregations frequently sing at other points in the service as well. All six denominations recommend a hymn at the beginning of the time of worship. This hymn often serves as a chance for the congregation to remind itself why it has assembled together in the first place. Such an opening hymn might point toward God's worthiness to be praised. Other hymns especially designated as appropriate for the opening of worship might foretell what will happen later in the service, as we see in verse 2 of "God is Here" by Fred Pratt Green:

> Here are symbols to remind us of our lifelong need of grace;
> here are table, font, and pulpit; here the cross has central place.
> Here in honesty of preaching, here in silence, as in speech,
> here, in newness and renewal, God the Spirit comes to each."[96]

Still other opening hymns allow the congregation to respond to the importance of Sunday in the plan of God's salvation story:

> This is the day the Lord hath made,
> that all may see his love displayed,
> may feel his resurrection pow'r,
> and rise again to fall no more,
> in perfect righteousness renewed
> and filled with all the life of God.[97]

Each of the worship orders mentioned above specifies using a hymn either before or in the middle of the scripture readings for the

---

[96] Fred Pratt Green, "God is Here," © 1979, Hope Publishing Company, Carol Stream, IL 60188. Used by permission.

[97] Charles Wesley, "Come, Let Us with Our Lord Arise," verse 2, in *Rejoice in the Lord* (Grand Rapids: Eerdmans Publishing Company, 1985), 512.

day.[98] This leaves room for the congregation to respond to a specific reading, as described previously, or to affirm the importance of the scriptures in the Christian life. This hymn might express eagerness to receive wisdom from the Word, as we find in an old Lutheran chorale:

> Blessed Jesus, at your word
> we are gathered here to hear you.
> Let our hearts and souls be stirred
> now to seek and love and fear you.
> By your gospel pure and holy;
> teach us, Lord, to love you solely.[99]

Or the congregation might sing a prayer for guidance in understanding the Biblical texts read that day, as we find in Charles Wesley's text:

> Come, Holy Ghost (for moved by thee
> the prophets wrote and spoke),
> unlock the truth, thyself the key,
> unseal the sacred book.[100]

Another likely location for a hymn is during or immediately following the offering. The term "offering," found in hymnal indices and tables of contents, refers worship leaders to texts that give voice to the congregation's gratitude and recognition that all things come from God alone. These texts help the congregation to offer up its gifts, in language both ancient ("accept the gifts we offer, for all thy love imparts, and

---

[98] *Evangelical Lutheran Worship* recommends an appropriate hymn, an alleluia, or some other sung acclamation in order to welcome the Gospel reading.

[99] Tobias Clausnitzer, "Blessed Jesus, at Your Word," verse 1, trans. Catherine Winkworth. Found in *Psalter Hymnal* (Grand Rapids: CRC Publications, 1987), 280.

[100] Charles Wesley, "Come, Holy Ghost, Our Hearts Inspire," verse 2. Found in *The United Methodist Hymnal*, 603.

what thou most desirest, our humble, thankful hearts")[101] and modern ("What gift can we bring, what present, what token? What words can convey it, the joy of this day?").[102]

Finally, five of the six orders for worship mentioned above include a hymn either before or after the benediction. This is the location of the hymn that Jesus sang with his disciples in Matthew 26:30, at the end of their Seder celebration. At this time, the congregation can respond to all that has happened during the past hour or more, and can affirm its commitment to live lives shaped by the God encountered in worship. These desires may be voiced to each other, as wishes for each member of the congregation, which we find in the hymn "God Be with You Till we Meet Again."[103] Or they may be expressed as a final prayer directly to God, as in "Lord, as We Rise to Leave the Shell of Worship."[104]

The structure of hymnals themselves also shows this responsive function of hymns. Hymnals are nearly universally organized by topic, with hymns usually grouped in ways that recognize the Trinity (separate sections for hymns to the Father, Son, and Spirit) as well as the life of Christ (with hymns arranged in order of the church year, from Advent, through Christmas, Epiphany, a section on Christ's life or ministry, Holy Week, and finally Easter, culminating in Pentecost). Other hymns fall into categories concerning their use in worship

---

[101] Matthias Claudius, "We Plow the Fields and Scatter," verse 3, trans. Jane Montgomery-Campbell, in *Rejoice in the Lord*, 17.

[102] Jane Marshall, "What Gift Can We Bring," verse 1, in *The United Methodist Hymnal*, 87.

[103] Jeremiah E. Rankin, "God Be with You Till We Meet Again," in *Psalter Hymnal*, 316.

[104] Fred Kaan, "Lord, as We Rise to Leave the Shell of Worship," in *Rejoice in the Lord*, 513.

(morning and evening hymns, baptismal and Eucharistic hymns, etc) and the way in which they relate to Christian living (evangelism hymns, social justice hymns, etc). Indices in the back of nearly all hymnals also point worship planners to texts that respond to feelings such as discouragement, issues such as race relations, and people groups such as youth.[105] This organizational structure makes plain the function of hymns as vehicles for response to scripture, worship, and the world around us.

THE UNIFYING ROLE OF HYMNS

While the text of a hymn invites the congregation to respond to various elements or ideas that occur in worship, the music to which these hymn texts are set serves to bind the congregation together. Although they are often disparaged as difficult by those who favor contemporary Christian music, hymn tunes were and are designed to be music for groups of amateur singers. Hymn tunes are short, rarely more than 16 measures long, and usually designed to be repeated several times so that what is unclear on the first verse becomes easy by the fourth. Such repetition particularly aids members of the congregation who cannot read music. Hymn tunes are also generally constrained in both their rhythms and their pitches. Congregational hymns rarely exceed a musical range of an octave by more than a step or two, since untrained voices do not typically have large ranges; neither do most congregations warm up their voices before singing hymns in worship. Likewise, most hymns are made up of strings of quarter notes, presenting simple rhythms that can be easily followed by untrained singers.

---

[105] All of these topics are taken from the Topical Index of *Rejoice in the Lord.*

When members of the congregation join together in singing a hymn, the sheer physicality of vocal production helps them come together. When we sing together, we breathe together and we are all gathered in the same rhythm of inhaling and exhaling. Whether a congregation sings only the melody or sings in parts, the homophonic sound created provides an aural testimony to the unity of the Body of Christ. As Alice Parker writes, "the singers give up ego, selfhood, and control to enter that world of "vibration."[106] Such unity may even extend beyond the boundaries of time to knit together singing Christians of all generations. The quotation from Jean Janzen at the beginning of this chapter highlights this ability of music to bind together the physical and spiritual experiences of those who sing, no matter where or even when. Martin Luther acknowledged the ability of music to unify the Church throughout the ages in his commentary to Psalm 118: "When I look at all the saints, especially in the New Testament, the story is the same. I can hear voices of rejoicing in their tabernacles, joyous songs and hymns of salvation and victory, of the help of God. And we sing along and join in the praise and thanks, just as we are one in our faith and trust in God and also share in suffering."[107]

Joseph Gelineau expresses the foundation of this unity:

[Worship] is the shared activity of a people gathered together. No other sign brings out this communal dimension so well as singing. Bodily movements can be synchronized but remain juxtaposed. Many individual voices, however, can actually be fused together, so that when they blend and follow the same rhythm, only one voice is heard – that of the group. This brings out a very strong feeling of unity and of belonging. It even

---

[106] Alice Parker, *Melodious Accord: Good Singing in the Church* (Chicago: Liturgy Training Publications, 1991), 117.

[107] Martin Luther, *Commentary on Psalm 118*, cited by Carl Schalk, *Luther on Music: Paradigms of Praise* (St. Louis: Concordia, 1988), 48.

72

touches on the essential mystery of the Church as *koinonia*. From the time of Ignatius of Antioch down to our own day, singing with one voice has remained a privileged way of expressing unity in diversity.[108]

The "fused" sound that Gelineau describes not only helps congregations to feel a sense of unity, but it allows them to enact that unity through their vocal participation. Thus congregational singing becomes a powerful symbol of the unity of the Body of Christ. Paul Tillich describes a symbol as that which points beyond itself to something else, participates in the nature of that to which it points, and reveals "levels of reality" that are not accessible in other ways.[109] Tillich's definition helps us see that congregational singing reminds us of the unity of the Body of Christ, allows us to participate in that unity, and reveals it in ways that help us understand it better.

SCRIPTURAL INSTANCES OF THE RESPONSORY ROLE OF MUSIC

Gelineau's eloquent testimony to the power of music to enhance, reflect, and enact unity among worshippers points to the numerous New Testament scripture passages that speak to the goal of peace and accord in the Church. In his letter to the church in Ephesus, the apostle Paul encourages such agreement:

---

[108] Joseph Gelineau, "Music and Singing in the Liturgy," in *The Study of Liturgy*, ed. Cheslyn Jones, Geoffrey Wainwright, Edward Yarnold, and Paul Bradshaw (New York: Oxford University Press, 1992), 495.

[109] Paul Tillich, *Dynamics of Faith* (New York: Harper & Brothers Publishers, 1957), 41-42.

I therefore, the prisoner in the Lord, beg you to lead a life worthy of the calling to which you have been called, with all humility and gentleness, with patience, bearing with one another in love, making every effort to maintain the unity of the Spirit in the bond of peace. There is one body and one Spirit, just as you were called to the one hope of your calling, one Lord, one faith, one baptism, one God and Father of all, who is above all and through all and in all. (Eph 4:1-6)

We see similar instructions in Romans 12:4-5, 1 Corinthians 10:17, 1 Corinthians 12:12-13, Colossians 3:12-15, and 1 Peter 3:8. These passages seem to uphold the goal of unity, expressed often as having one mind, or one heart, or one faith. Hymn-singing congregations affirm and aspire to such unity, which they express by singing with one voice.

Other verses provide evidence of the use of hymn texts as congregational responses to scripture and to worship. In 1 Corinthians 14, Paul instructs that all prayers and blessings must be able to be interpreted in the vernacular. Otherwise, he explains, members of the congregation will not be able to say their "amen" to what has been said. Paul assumes that after an individual offering of words or prayers, the entire congregation is invited to respond with its approval by adding "amen" to what has been said. This glimpse into first-century worship shows that the use of congregational responses, whether sung or spoken, whether brief or extended, goes back to our earliest ancestors in the faith of Christ.

The New Testament also includes several references to hymns. Jesus and his disciples sang a hymn at the conclusion of their Last Supper, as mentioned earlier. Paul and Silas sang many hymns together while in prison in Acts 16:25; these seem to be communal hymns in the way we understand the term. The hymn mentioned in 1 Corinthians 14:26, however, appears to be a different sort of song. This verse

74

mentions a hymn synonymous with revelations, interpretations, and lessons offered by one person to the whole congregation. We will speak more of such individual or personal "hymns" in the next chapter.

The most famous account of hymns in the New Testament is Paul's list of "psalms and hymns and spiritual songs," found in Ephesians 5:19 and Colossians 3:16. Scholars have debated the specific meanings of the three musical terms Paul uses, a scholarly discussion that Paul Westermeyer admirably records in *Te Deum*. He notes that although some believe that Paul's three terms point to songs used in different ways, most scholars find that the terms are used interchangeably.[110] Despite the confusion over Paul's musical terminology, we can glean some general understanding of his goals in writing. Although the contexts of these phrases seem to be different (the letter to the Ephesians warning against unwise living and the letter to the Colossians affirming holy camaraderie), these mentions of hymns have two things in common. First, each passage takes for granted communal singing; to the Ephesians, Paul writes that such singing is to be done "among yourselves," while to the believers in Colossae, Paul couches the passage in praise of unity and communal support. Secondly, in each instance, the singing of hymns and other songs serves as a grateful response to God. Singing is the Christian's reply, allowing the community to "give thanks" for all that it has seen and heard and known of God's great goodness.

---

[110] Paul Westermeyer, *Te Deum: The Church and Music* (Minneapolis: Fortress Press, 1998), 59. Westermeyer consults scholars including Christian Hannick, Margot Fassler, Peter Jeffrey, Lawrence A. Hoffman, Janet R. Walton, James McKinnon, Robert A. Skeris, and Egon Wellesz in his thorough survey of literature on this topic.

CRITICISM OF THE RESPONSIVE USE OF MUSIC IN HYMN SINGING

Over the past several decades, hymn singing has attracted much criticism. Much of that criticism is sparked by an evangelical desire to attract people to worship. In hopes of making worship more appealing to those who do not currently belong to a church, these critics find that the style of music of most hymns denotes an old-fashioned, "churchy" atmosphere that sounds dated and inaccessible to modern people. This complaint contains much truth. Despite the fact that hymns themselves have been used historically to attract converts to opportunities for worship, very little contemporary music employs the homophonic style of hymns, save for many national anthems (which are, themselves, generally quite old).[111] Fans of jazz, rock, country, pop, Broadway, and even classical music do not see their musical preferences reflected in the tunes of most hymns.

Secondly, these critics suggest that hymns are difficult to sing. Despite the fact that hymn tunes have been written from the very beginning for use by amateur musicians, without rehearsal, those unfamiliar with hymns commonly complain that they are confusing. This criticism is somewhat more difficult to receive than the first, which had obvious roots in truth. What makes hymns difficult to sing? When their rhythms are generally simple and their melodies are straight-forward and repeated several times, what problems do they pose to the average singer? I believe the answer to these questions lies in familiarity, and stems from the question above. Not only do many

---

[111] The hymns of Charles Wesley provide an example of how enthusiastic singing of emotional texts drew many to join in the singing. Wesley wrote in part from an evangelical desire to foster and encourage those attempting to live out their faith. See Carlton R. Young, *Music of the Heart: John and Charles Wesley on Music and Musicians* (Carol Stream, Illinois: Hope, 1995), 27-32.

people today not choose to listen to hymn-style music outside of church, they often also do not hear hymns during worship. When they thus encounter a new hymn, the overriding experience of foreignness blocks any desire or ability to learn or sing it. For those unused to the homophonic progression of the musical language of hymns, nearly any hymn might provoke such a reaction. The singer indeed experiences the hymn as difficult and confusing, however it is not usually the hymn tune per se, but the reaction of the singer that truly makes it so.

If we look at hymn texts, this complaint seems more understandable. Hymn texts are poems dense with meaning. Hymns that were written centuries, or even decades, ago use terms that may be unusual and incomprehensible to modern ears and minds. How many singers have wondered what an "Ebenezer" was ("Come Thou Fount of Every Blessing")? Had not George Whitefield had the good sense to edit Wesley's beloved Christmas hymn, we would sing "Hark! How all the welkin rings" and likewise wonder what a welkin might be.[112] Although newer hymns have generally simpler and more familiar language, older hymns frequently present problems.[113]

Finally, another critique of hymns arises out of their very nature. If hymns do indeed respond to scripture readings and worship actions, then they do not necessarily need to be addressed to God. They might

---

[112] Young, *Companion*, 387.

[113] And this problem, in turn, raises another problem. Hymnal editors have long engaged in updating hymn texts, to replace phrases that are no longer understood as well as to alter usages which offend modern sensibilities, such as language which assumes that both singer and God are male. These editors attempt to maintain a difficult balance between honoring the author's intentions, making the hymn text accessible to modern understanding, keeping up with current liturgical and theological practices, and ministering to those whose faith is enmeshed with archaic language from the original text.

restate a Biblical verse or two, or they may be sung to encourage the entire congregation in faithful living. Many hymns are, indeed, sung directly to God, but this is not a requirement of the genre. Some worship planners feel that it ought to be. Those who believe that music in worship should consist of direct communication to God are necessarily disappointed when their assumptions do not coincide with all hymns. Hymns can be thus experienced as preventing Christians from directly addressing God.

INTRODUCING THIS FUNCTION INTO THE WORSHIP OF OTHER TRADITIONS

Congregations that do not belong to a hymn-singing tradition may still want to incorporate some of this responsorial use of music in their worship services. There are several ways to attempt this, and I have included two suggestions for using music that facilitate congregation response in worship.

The Lutheran Church has a tradition of identifying a "hymn of the week" – a selection that is chosen to react to the scripture readings of the day, especially the gospel reading. Other hymns during the worship service may function in other ways, but the "hymn of the week" serves as a vehicle for the congregation to interact with and respond to the themes of the Gospel reading for each Sunday.[114] No matter what style of music is employed in worship, the leaders of a congregation can choose one piece specifically to allow the congregation to respond to the scripture or theme of the day, and that music can be placed immediately

---

[114] See Erik Routley, *Music Leadership in the Church* (Nashville: Abingdon, 1967), 104. The Lutheran Church encouraged its members to sing these hymns at home during the week as well as on Sundays in worship.

following the sermon. In this way, the congregation, rather than the pastor or preacher, is given the "last word," and its response is validated by placing the singing in such an important location within the service.

Another option for using music as a response involves more active congregational participation as well as more advance preparation. Leaders might encourage members of the congregation with skill in written expression to craft responses to each week's readings or topics. These new "hymns" could be written to employ familiar melodies that the congregation already knows, or musicians in the congregation could craft new melodies for the new texts. In either case, this plan allows the congregation to respond to the matter of worship in two ways: by writing musical responses and also by singing them. Although such stepping out in faith may require some coaxing and practice, a congregation would gain much from being able to offer its own sentiments in its own voice.

A hymn-singing congregation uses this musical form to respond to scripture, sermon, worship, and life in a unified expression of faith. Hymns bind the congregation together even as they give the congregation's understanding voice. Yet those musical forms that have been excluded from hymnals present new and different ways to use music in worship. The next chapter will describe how gospel songs, so easily dismissed by hymnal editors, function as vehicles of personal testimony.

Chapter 4: Singing in the Gospel Tradition
Song as Testimony

For days before I wrote this hymn, all had seemed dark to me. This was an unusual experience, for I have always been most cheerful; and so in my human weakness I cried in prayer, "Dear Lord, hold Thou my hand." Almost at once the sweet peace that comes of perfect assurance returned to my heart, and my gratitude for this instance of answered prayer sang itself in the lines of the hymn.[115]

The weight of souls was on them... they felt it their immediate duty therefore, most earnestly, and even passionately, to warn, to counsel, to entreat, to admonish, to reprove, to win them by the Love of Christ to be reconciled to God.[116]

As mentioned in the last chapter, Christians have not always considered all sung texts to be hymns. This chapter will take up the subject of Gospel songs, a category broad enough to include pieces sung at the camp meetings and revivals of the early 1800s as well as the works of writers such as Fanny Crosby and Ira Sankey later in that century.

All of the examples of music and text within this broad category have several things in common. First, they use simple words to convey a

---

[115] Fanny Crosby, *Memories of Eighty Years* (Boston: James H. Earle & Company, 1906), 171.

[116] William Henry Milburn, *The Lance, Cross, and Canoe* (New York: Thompson, 1892), 350-351. Quoted in Charles A. Johnson, *The Frontier Camp Meeting* (Dallas: Southern Methodist University Press, 1955), 173.

straightforward message. The intended audience for this body of music was often illiterate, unfamiliar with Christianity, or both. Texts, therefore, needed to be easy to understand. Subtle concepts of Christian theology gave way in these verses to broad and attractive descriptions of salvation and gratitude.

Texts also needed to be memorable. Frequently, repeated tag lines or choruses were included so that those without hymnals or the ability to read them could quickly memorize a refrain and participate.[117] Song leaders added familiar "floating choruses" to many different hymns, whether or not the music and the text or these two disparate compositions elided smoothly. For example, "Come, We that Love the Lord," a hymn by Isaac Watts, acquired the chorus "Marching to Zion," written by Robert Lowry. While this pair works together fairly well, aided by Lowry's musical composition that unifies the two texts, "Alas! And did my Savior Bleed," another Watts text, did not fare so well. This mournful and contemplative text became yoked to a chorus by Ralph Hudson with the following text: "At the cross, at the cross, where I first saw the light, and the burden of my heart rolled away; it was there by faith I received my sight, and now I am happy all the day." Modern-day singers experience musical whiplash alternating between Watt's penitential gratitude and the cheerful text and jaunty melody of Hudson's chorus. Whether such discontinuity troubled the first singers of this hybrid hymn text is unknown.

Music was likewise simple. Most revival and gospel hymns used a minimum of chords, making them playable by the least skilled of musicians. These simple pieces were invariably found in major keys,

---

[117] Harry Eskew and Hugh T. McElrath, *Sing with Understanding: An Introduction to Christian Hymnody*, 2nd ed. (Nashville: Church Street Press, 1995), 185-186.

echoing the optimistic texts. And musicians created melodies that were catchy and repetitive, so that they could be learned quickly by song leaders and congregations alike.

Finally, these songs relied on emotional appeal. They were created to express the enthusiastic fervor of the Christian, a passion that would draw the unconverted to a closer walk with God. Both music and texts aided in communicating feelings as an important component of what it means to be a Christian; not only should Christians believe certain things or act in certain ways, but they should also experience appropriate emotions. Lyrics expressed these feelings of gratitude and love toward God, and sorrow at the fate of the unconverted, while melodies heightened the emotional appeal of the words with sentimental musical phrases. Authors bolstered the rhetorical appeal of their songs by justifying their calls to repentance or conversion with heart-felt and personal experience rather than theology. Indeed, weighty theological reasons may have seemed too complicated or too remote to the authors for their intended audience.

HISTORY AND ANTECEDENTS OF GOSPEL SONGS

Although gospel songs and related musical forms flowered during the nineteenth century, earlier forms of congregational song foreshadowed many of the techniques used by the creators of gospel songs, including musical and ideological simplicity and subjective, emotional language rather than objective theological language. The last of these points appears vividly in the pietistic hymns of Lutheran and Reformed European churches.

Pietism arose in the seventeenth century, in part to counter a lifeless adherence to tradition that critics felt had developed in the Protestant Churches. Those critics feared that religion had become calcified into a system of rules one must obey and theological precepts to which one must assent. They desired that Christians should instead attend to their feelings and their lives, their inner experiences of faith and the ways in which they lived out those experiences daily.

The movement is particularly associated with Philipp Jacob Spener, who wrote *Pia Desideria* as an introduction to Pietist ideals. These included "conversion, new birth, and sanctification," as well as attention to private devotion and public missions.[118] Such foci resulted in hymns that expressed an individual and emotional response to God for the work of Jesus Christ. These new texts contrasted sharply with the orthodox hymns of the Lutheran Church, which maintained a collective stance rather than an individual perspective. Johann Jakob Schutz, Lutheran poet and friend of Spener, reflects this tender, Pietistic approach in the first verse of one of his hymns: "with healing balm my soul he fills and ev'ry faithless murmur stills: to God all praise and glory!"[119] The Pietist movement spread also to the Reformed Church in Germany, where it inspired authors including Joachim Neander to create more hymns. Neander's best-known text shares with Spener's a concern with displaying the all-powerful God's care for fragile humanity. Although God is "King of creation," this tender Lord also "shieldeth thee gently from harm" and "with his love doth befriend thee."[120]

---

[118] Hans-Christoph Schmidt-Lauber, "The Lutheran Tradition in the German Lands," in *The Oxford History of Christian Worship*, ed. Geoffrey Wainwright and Karen B. Westerfield Tucker (New York: Oxford University Press, 2006), 407.

[119] Johann Jakob Schutz, "Sing Praise to God Who Reigns Above," tr. Frances E. Cox in *Rejoice in the Lord* (Grand Rapids: Eerdmans, 1985), 146.

[120] Joachim Neander, "Praise to the Lord, the Almighty," tr. Catherine Winkworth in *Rejoice in the Lord*, 145.

As a side note, many scholars of religion and music have examined the question of whether J. S. Bach would be better considered a Pietist or an orthodox Lutheran.[121] Gunther Stiller firmly asserts that Bach found his theological and spiritual home within the liturgical life of the orthodox Lutheran church, citing his participation at the Eucharist, the manner in which his cantatas proclaim the gospel, and his compositional use of chorale tunes.[122] Yet the emotional fervor that the Pietists encouraged seems present in the music of Bach as well; one could list countless examples of moments in his cantatas and passions when Bach uses musical means to express the feelings he seems to want to create in his listeners.

Such concentration on the relationship between God and the individual, and on the emotional reaction that this relationship should spark, became evident once again in some of the hymns of Charles Wesley. Wesley could write texts full of the theology of the early Church Fathers as wells as hymns bursting with scriptural allusions. But part of his interest and appeal was in crafting personal expressions of gratitude that the Lord of the Universe could love and forgive him. We see this in one of the texts Charles Wesley wrote about his conversion experience,

---

[121] See the dissertations "The Bach Cantatas and Spenerian Pietism" by Thomas Jackson Bell, "Bach and Pietism" by Hans Ludwig Holborn, "Insights into Johann Sebastian Bach's Theology" by Paul S. Jones, "The Dialogue Movements in Bach Cantatas: a Preliminary Investigation into the Possible Influence of Eighteenth-Century Pietism on the Music of Johann Sebastian Bach" by Mark William Knoll, "Spenerian Pietism and the Cantatas of Johann Sebastian Bach" by Ray Alonzo Reed, and "The Theological Influence of the Pietist Movement on the Texts of Bach's Sacred Cantatas" by June Lee Saler. In general, these studies judge that both Lutheran orthodoxy and Pietism contributed to the formation of Bach's spirituality, theology, and music.

[122] Gunther Stiller, *Johann Sebastian Bach and Liturgical Life in Leipzig*, trans Herbert J.A. Bouman, Daniel F. Poellot, and Hilton C. Oswald (St. Louis: Concordia, 1984), 200-256.

"And Can it Be that I Should Gain."[123] In this poem, Wesley probes his own sinful nature ("my imprisoned spirit lay fast bound in sin and nature's night"), God's gracious interest in the individual ("How can it be that thou, my Lord, shouldst die for me?"), and the joy of his resulting conversion ("No condemnation now I dread... bold I approach th'eternal throne, and claim the crown, through Christ").[124]

Yet the hymns of the Wesleyan movement, like those of Pietism a century before, were only precursors to the Gospel songs that would spring forth a century later. Neander and Schutz wrote for educated singers who could purchase and sing from published collections of their hymns. And although many of Wesley's hymns were taken up by the poor and uneducated to whom both Charles and his brother John preached, the hymns themselves reflect a profound depth of scriptural, theological, and liturgical understanding.[125] The hymns of all three

---

[123] Carlton R. Young, *Companion to the United Methodist Hymnal* (Nashville: Abingdon, 1993), 212.

[124] Charles Wesley, "And Can it Be that I Should Gain" in *Rejoice in the Lord*, 451.

[125] Erik Routley describes Wesley's verses as "a hymnic output which is unmatched anywhere in the literature for volume, variety, and distinction of style... [Despite such a large output of hymns] what a high standard of doctrine, eloquence, and lyricism he reaches in so many of them... Not infrequently he is didactic, but he is hardly anything but ecstatic. Such a pressure of devotion needed the discipline of doctrine, and this we find in him to a degree that is the measure of his outstanding preeminence among evangelicals. The simplest and most "popular" of his hymns... abound in scriptural echoes and allusions; the profoundest abound equally..." Ultimately, Routley finds such a scholastic level to be a minor drawback in the reception of Wesley's hymns. Comparing him to Isaac Watts, Routley finds that "Watts uses less 'in-group' language; perhaps at his best he is more public [than Wesley], easier to offer to Christians whose faith is not learned or intense. Wesley is much more for those who have traveled far." *A Panorama of Christian Hymnody*, ed. Paul A. Richardson, (Chicago: GIA, 2005), 57-58.

authors balanced emotion with theology, and did not shy away from subtle concepts or challenging vocabulary.

Poets of the eighteenth century followed in the footsteps of Pietist hymn-writers and Charles Wesley, writing "hymns of personal devotion" that emphasized the individual's experience of faith, often communicated in emotional terms.[126] Erik Routley even finds some traces of "emphases on the personal rather than the public," which he sees as one trait of romanticism, within the work and hymn texts of the Oxford Movement, known for its love of Gothic aesthetics and early Greek and Latin Christian hymns.[127] Well-known hymn texts such as "In the Cross of Christ I Glory," "Abide with Me! Fast Falls the Eventide," and "Just as I Am" arose in this movement conducive to emotional and personal texts. Yet only in the rough frontier of early nineteenth-century America did the simple appeal of the Gospel song coalesce into an entirely new art form.

This process began as part of the Second Great Awakening. People in rural areas of the United States gathered for camp meetings that would last several days. These camp meetings provided a unique opportunity for white and black Americans, both free and enslaved, to share in religious experiences. Although it would be anachronistic to read a twenty-first century desire for equality into nineteenth century events, Albert J. Raboteau describes the camp meetings' tentative

---

[126] Eskew and McElrath, 148-151.

[127] Routley, 95. Routley finds these Romantic roots in Methodism, as he wonderfully contrasts to followers of John Calvin: "There is much about the Wesleyan enterprise that is Romantic: the sheer adventure of it all; all that traveling; the exposure of evangelists to danger; the pursuit of a far-off but always visible goal; and the free reign given to personal expressions of religion. Wesley does not suspect Nature quite as deeply as a faithful Calvinist must."

openness to all: "The individualistic emphasis of revivalism, with its intense concentration on inward conversion, fostered an inclusiveness which could border on egalitarianism. Evangelicals did not hesitate to preach the necessity of conversion to racially mixed congregations."[128] Music played a crucial role at these gatherings. According to Karen Westerfield Tucker,

> The songs might come from denominational hymnals or out of camp meeting songsters produced by denominational editors or by independent compilers that stressed themes of repentance, judgment, and the benefits of heaven. Spontaneous songs or choruses could also erupt that might be repeated at future meetings, and an independent and new refrain could be added to a well-known existing hymn text... The presence at the camp meeting of persons of different ethnic and racial backgrounds provided an occasion for the sharing and mingling of musical forms, influencing the development, for example, of white and black spirituals. The camp in effect was a nursery for the gospel style of church song that became widespread in the late nineteenth-century.[129]

As Westerfield Tucker describes, a variety of musical forms appeared in camp meeting worship. Traditional hymns were sung, but those that highlighted individual experience found greatest use. Charles Johnson found that "religious ballads" frequently appeared at the revival. "Composed for individual singing, those narrating biblical happenings

---

[128] Albert J. Raboteau, *Slave Religion: The "Invisible Institution" in the Antebellum South* (New York, Oxford University Press, 1978), 132. Raboteau goes on to describe several African-Americans, both slave and free, who not only participated in camp meetings but preached to black, white, and mixed congregations, including Harry Hosier, Josiah (or Jacob) Bishop, William Lemon, Joseph Willis, and others.

[129] Karen B. Westerfield Tucker, "North America" in *The Oxford History of Christian Worship*, 606.

were strong favorites… A not uncommon twist was the addition of one's own personal religious experiences after a narration from the Scriptures… This type was extremely popular during the early nineteenth century when camp meeting altar services were introduced."[130]

Johnson also describes the "movement toward the folk level" that happened as "verses were shortened, refrains added, and expressions and ejaculations interpolated."[131] This process produced what he calls the "revival spiritual," a musical form of short verses and repetitive choruses that all could remember and sing. Even more reduction, and no small amount of improvisation, provided "the song of one short phrase repeated three or four times, and then followed by a one-phrase refrain." As an example of this minimalist form, Johnson mentions the song, "Oh, where is good old Noah? Oh, where is good old Noah? Oh, where is good old Noah? Safe in the promised land."[132]

But these musical forms and tendencies did not remain static. They continued to evolve into what came to be known as the gospel song, sometimes called "white" gospel to distinguish it from the African-American gospel tradition of the twentieth century. Such a differentiation is not entirely accurate, as African-American participants, both slave and free, contributed greatly to the evolution of the gospel song. To call these songs "white" gospel deceptively conceals their true

---

[130] Johnson, 196-197. Charles A. Johnson, *The Frontier Camp Meeting: Religion's Harvest Time* (Dallas: Southern Methodist University Press, 1955), 196-197. Notice the similarities between this description and Charles Wesley's hymn "Wrestling Jacob," discussed in the previous chapter.

[131] Johnson, 201.

[132] Ibid., 202.

origin in the intersection of musical styles from descendants of European and African cultures.

The gospel style burst into prominence due to several other influences besides the impact of camp meetings. The growth of urban Sunday Schools in the mid-nineteenth century required music appropriate for adults and children learning about the Christian faith. Urban revivals also echoed the excitement and evangelism that occurred in their earlier rural cousins, the camp meetings. Both of these movements sought music and texts that would attract newcomers and express the simplest tenets of Christianity.

Gospel composers took their cue from contemporary musical styles. Popular at the time were the graceful and sentimental ballads of Stephan C. Foster, songs that conveyed a tender emotionalism best expressed when sung by a soloist. Carlton Young notices similarity in music and in attitude between Foster's "I Dream of Jeanie with the Light Brown Hair" and two popular Gospel songs, "Jesus, Savior, Pilot Me" and "What a Friend We Have in Jesus."[133] Other Gospel songs favored military-style marches with rousing choruses, as heard in songs like "Standing on the Promises" and "Leaning on the Everlasting Arms."[134] William Bradbury, a notable composer of Gospel tunes, borrowed both of these styles when writing music for Sunday School hymns, including "Jesus Loves Me" and "My Hope is Built on Nothing Less."[135]

---

[133] Carlton R. Young, *My Great Redeemer's Praise: An Introduction to Christian Hymns* (Akron: OSL Publications, 1995), 95.

[134] Ibid., 96.

[135] **Eskew and McElrath, 196-197.**

89

One of the most prolific authors of Gospel song texts, Fanny Crosby began writing poems by the time she was six years old. She went on to scribe more than 8,500 Gospel songs during her long life, despite the constraints of being a blind woman in the nineteenth century. Her texts, which include "Pass Me Not, O Gentle Savior," "To God be the Glory," "Jesus, Keep Me Near the Cross," and "Blessed Assurance," exhibit the common themes of Gospel songs: reaching out to the unsaved, depending on God who, through Jesus, saves us despite our weakness, gratitude and confidence in response to salvation, and anticipating heaven, where proximity to God will provide even more joy.[136]

Another important composer and author of Gospel songs, Charles Albert Tindley, personified the interweavings of African-American influence on the genre. Tindley's parents were both slaves, and he grew up to become ordained in the Methodist Church and pastor a large multicultural congregation in Philadelphia.[137] His contributions to the gospel genre include "By and By (We are Tossed and Driven)," "Nothing Between my Soul and my Savior," "When the Storms of Life are Raging, Stand by Me," and "Take Your Burden to the Lord and Leave it There." In addition to maintaining an important place in the repertoire of Gospel songs, Tindley's work paved the way for later developments in African-American religious music. In the words of scholar Robert Darden,

> the songs of C. A. Tindley – and only about fifty are known to exist – differ significantly from the hymns of popular white composers such as William B. Bradbury, Fanny J. Crosby, and

---

[136] Young, *My Great Redeemer's Praise*, 96-97.

[137] Robert Darden, *People Get Ready! A New History of Black Gospel Music* (New York: Continuum, 2004), 160-161.

William Howard Doane. Tindley's lyrics focused instead on specific concerns of African-American Christians... Furthermore, most of his songs were placed in the pentatonic scale and allowed ample room for rhythmic, melodic, and even lyric improvisations.[138]

Darden is wrong to list Crosby with composers Bradbury and Doane, as she was an author of texts rather than a tunesmith. Yet he states correctly that Bradbury and Doane include all scale degrees in their melodies, distinguishing their compositions from Tindley's pentatonic, proto-blues melodies. Both his musical embrace of the pentatonic scale and his willingness to confront the difficulties of African-American life make Tindley "the first gospel hymn writer to have considerable influence on black gospel song writers."[139]

Gospel songs were used extensively at revivals, traveling evangelism programs, and Sunday Schools. For many decades, however, they rarely found a place at Sunday morning worship. These lively and emotional songs were linked too closely with their rough beginnings at camp meetings and on city streets to feature in genteel Sunday worship services. The melodies of these gospel songs too closely resembled secular tunes inappropriate to be hinted at during worship. With the beginning of the twentieth century, however, evangelical denominations began to incorporate the singing of Gospel songs into the music of their Sunday services. New Gospel authors and composers continued to write in this genre. "Great is Thy Faithfulness" and "He Lives" come from the first half of the twentieth century, while musicians such as the Gaithers continue to create Gospel songs today.[140] The Gospel song's qualities of

---

[138] Ibid.

[139] Melva Wilson Costen, *In Spirit and In Truth: The Music of African American Worship* (Louisville: Westminster John Knox, 2004), 82-83.

[140] Eskew and McElrath, 204.

simplicity, emotional openness, and appeal in both text and music have profoundly influenced the contemporary praise and worship music of many congregations, a topic that will be explored in the next chapter.

The guiding principles of the Gospel song, a simple personal and emotional plea set to music drawing from secular idioms, seemed to reappear in a different guise in African-American gospel music of the twentieth and twenty-first centuries. This repertoire began to form as millions of former slaves moved north in search of increased opportunity during the Great Migration. These newcomers found themselves excluded from both white communities and Northern African-American communities, which tended to look down upon their rural and illiterate Southern peers. African-Americans new to the North found solace in Pentecostal and Holiness congregations, where worship music employed a rich combination of African-American secular musical styles such as ragtime, jazz, and blues, as well as the instruments usually associated with such music: pianos, guitars, and percussion. African-American gospel music arose from these roots, marrying the exciting music of secular Black culture with the religious content of the spirituals. Although the harmonic and rhythmic language of this gospel music sound nothing like the sentimental harmonies and restrained melodies of Foster-esque Gospel songs, the practice of combining appealing secular musical styles with lyrics about salvation connects these two repertoires. Likewise, African-American Gospel music often incorporates the same relational language, first-person singular grammatical construction, emotional intensity, and desire to share the good news that one finds in Gospel songs. Gospel music flourishes, as artists such as Kirk Franklin, Israel Houghton, and Mary Mary follow in the footsteps of Gospel innovators Thomas Andrew Dorsey and Mahalia Jackson.

Not only do new Gospel songs continue to be written, but old Gospel songs continue to be sung, even in churches that rarely sing hymns. Congregations that sing primarily praise and worship music are far more likely to turn to Gospel songs for occasional hymns than they are to Lutheran chorales or even the beautiful modern texts of twentieth and twenty-first century hymn writers.[141] A certain irony exists in the fact that Gospel songs, which were long considered different from and inferior to real hymns, have now become the best-known examples of "hymns" in many modern congregations.

THE TESTIMONIAL FUNCTION OF GOSPEL SONG TEXTS

As mentioned before, Gospel songs were created to be sung by an individual. As such, these songs function as testimonies. A testimony is

> an individual person's faith story that is told to others. Testimonies tend to address one of two topics: Either they explain how and why people converted to their current expression of faith, or they describe extraordinary occurrences in people's lives that strengthened or restored their faith commitment... Intrinsically motivational, a good testimony reinforces the religious commitment of the person telling the

---

[141] I have found that my church music history students, who come largely from mid-west evangelical Christian backgrounds, evidence familiarity with very few hymn texts and tunes. When this class comes to music of the revivals and gospel hymnody, however, many finally recognize a number of the texts and tunes we study. Moreover, these gospel songs are often featured by contemporary Christian musicians. A 2014 Youtube playlist entitled "Old Hymns by Modern Artists" includes the Gospel songs "Blessed Assurance," "'Tis So Sweet to Trust in Jesus," "Great is Thy Faithfulness," "How Great Thou Art," "Grace Greater than All Our Sin," "Because He Lives," "Nothing But the Blood of Jesus," and "Jesus Paid it All." The number of examples of other genres of hymnody (chorales, Oxford movement hymns, twentieth century hymnody, metrical psalms, etc) is negligible.

story while moving those who hear it toward analogous behavior.[142]

Carlton Young describes this function in the original use of Gospel songs: "In its most compelling form, the faith story to be preached was sung by a soloist or the choir and the congregation without the prop of a hymnal. Most in the congregation could not read either the words or music, and they sang only the refrain as they came forward in response to the call."[143] The individual nature and first-person singular grammatical construction of Gospel lyrics allowed them to serve as personal evidence of God's grace, salvation, power, and love. When sung by a single person, that "faith story" becomes both testimony of past action and a call to future action on the part of the congregation. By sharing his or her story, expressed in the words of a Gospel song, the soloist can summon listeners to look to God for salvation or for a renewed sense of faith.

That testimony might encapsulate the entire journey from sin to salvation, as we see in the twentieth-century Gospel song, "Freely, Freely:" "God forgave my sins in Jesus' name, I've been born again in Jesus' name, and in Jesus' name I come to you, to share his love as he told me to."[144] Sometimes that journey includes allusions to a final end in heaven as part of the story, as we find in "There's Within My Heart a Melody:"

> All my life was wrecked by sin and strife,
> discord filled my heart with pain;

---

[142] Brenda E. Brasher, "Testimony," in *Contemporary American Religion*, ed. Wade Clark Roof (New York: Macmillan Reference, 1999), 728.

[143] Young, *My Great Redeemer's Praise*, 93.

[144] Verse 1 of "Freely, Freely" by Carol Owens, as found in *The United Methodist Hymnal* (Nashville: United Methodist Publishing House, 1989), 389.

94

Jesus swept across the broken strings,
stirred the slumbering chords again.

Soon he's coming back to welcome me
far beyond the starry sky;
I shall wing my flight to worlds unknown;
I shall reign with him on high.[145]

Other songs present the soloist at a particular point on that journey. "Just as I Am, Without One Plea" shows us the individual's recognition of sinfulness and need. Songs such as "Pass Me Not, O Gentle Savior," and "I Surrender All" highlight the moment of prayer for forgiveness and salvation. The soloist explains that salvation and the feelings it produces in songs like "Nothing but the Blood," where "hope and peace" are the result of a saving encounter with Jesus. Salvation also prompts expressions of praise and gratitude, which some Gospel songs and many African-American Gospel musicians explore in depth. Donn Thomas provides an example of this in his 1997 song "Wailing into Dancing:"

You turned my wailing into dancing,
Took away my sadness and gave me joy.
You made my heart sing, I can't keep silent.
I will give you praise forever more.[146]

This encounter with God's grace leads to a desire to live a life worthy of repentance, which is expressed in "Where He Leads Me" and "Nothing Between." Finally, the singer may turn from an exploration of his or her own story to an outright appeal to the congregation. This call

---

[145] Luther Bridges, 1910, verses 2 and 5 as found in *The United Methodist Hymnal*, 380.

[146] "Wailing into Dancing," by Donn Thomas, © 2011 Maranatha Music. Found in *Zion Still Sings* (Nashville: Abingdon Press, 2007), 51. Used by permission.

appears explicitly in countless examples, such as "Softly and Tenderly Jesus is Calling," and "Only Trust Him:"

> Come, every soul by sin oppressed, there's mercy with the Lord;
> and he will surely give you rest, by trusting in his Word.
>
> Refrain: Only trust him, only trust him, only trust him now.
> He will save you, he will save you, he will save you now.
>
> For Jesus shed his precious blood rich blessings to bestow;
> plunge now into the crimson flood that washes bright as snow.
>
> Yes, Jesus is the truth, the way that leads you into rest;
> believe in him without delay, and you are fully blest.
>
> Come then and join this holy band, and on to glory go,
> to dwell in that celestial land where joys immortal flow. [147]

THE ATTRACTING ROLE OF GOSPEL MUSIC

As stated earlier, the music of the Gospel song reflected the intimacy, the solo performance practice, and the gentle sentimentality of popular parlor songs of the nineteenth century. The music functioned to make the words more appealing. Carlton Young believes that these "easily memorized tunes evoke the immediate response: 'Hey, they're (we're) singing my (our) song!'"[148] Gospel songs employed music that was so similar to the tunes present in everyday secular life that these melodies felt familiar even upon the first hearing. Even today, Gospel songs feel comfortable because they sound so typical. With their music already welcomed into the ears of their listeners, the texts of Gospel songs can likewise penetrate through any personal defenses aroused by foreign sounds and ideas.

---

[147] John H. Stockton, 1874. Found in *The United Methodist Hymnal*, 337.

[148] Young, *My Great Redeemer's Praise*, 93.

The similarity of Gospel tunes to secular musical styles provided a model for subsequent church music. As we will see in the next chapter, the practice of employing familiar sounds in order to attract listeners has continued and spread far beyond the genre of Gospel songs.

Simple tunes, such as those used with Gospel songs, are also remembered easily. This feature of the genre allows people who have heard a Gospel song only once or twice to recall the melody, and the words, of the song again effortlessly. This helps the message of the song to live on long after the original performance has finished, a secondary function of Gospel music.

SCRIPTURAL UNDERSTANDING OF THE TESTIMONIAL ROLE OF MUSIC

The words "testify" and "testimony" occur fairly frequently in the Bible. Often these terms carry a legal significance, connected with providing evidence at a trial. As an example of this usage, we find the high priest asking Jesus about the evidence of the false witnesses who testified against him (Matthew 26:62). Even outside of court, Biblical characters employ such legal language to discredit others or to prove their own honor. Samuel, in speaking to "all Israel" (1 Samuel 12), asks the people to testify against him in order to establish his righteousness and his credentials as a prophet.

Particularly in the New Testament, however, testimony takes on an expanded role – that of sharing the good news about Christ with others. The author of the Johannine epistles explains his understanding of the relationship between testimony and the Gospel in 1 John 5:6-12:

This is the one who came by water and blood, Jesus Christ, not with the water only but with the water and the blood. And the Spirit is the one that testifies, for the Spirit is the Truth. There are three that testify: the Spirit and the water and the blood, and these three agree. If we receive human testimony, the testimony of God is greater; for this is the testimony of God that he has testified to his Son. Those who believe in the Son of God have the testimony in their hearts. Those who do not believe in God have made him a liar by not believing in the testimony that God has given concerning his Son. And this is the testimony: God gave us eternal life, and this life is in his Son. Whoever has the Son has life; whoever does not have the Son of God does not have life.

Such a testimony is not visible evidence but internal witnessing (given by the third or the first person of the Trinity) that leads to belief. And such conviction as is gained through this testimony is then shared by testifying to others. We see that sharing elsewhere in the New Testament. In Acts 20:24, for example, Paul names his ministry as that of testifying to the good news of God's grace.

The concept of testifying or witnessing to the good news is far more prevalent in the Bible than the word itself, however. Time and time again, God instructs those who have entered into relationship with their Lord to "go and tell" others about God's power and love as evidenced in their own lives. The function of Gospel songs seems to cohere in many ways with the account of God's call to these individuals in the Bible. God commands Moses to explain the Passover celebration to children by saying "'It is because of what the Lord did for me when I came out of Egypt.'"[149] Interestingly, this phrase echoes the Gospel tendency toward singular pronouns and sharing one's own story, even though the entire nation of Israel was saved by the Passover event.

---

[149] Exodus 13:8, NRSV.

Likewise, the Psalms are full of declarations to God that the psalmist will "tell of your name to my brothers and sisters; in the midst of the congregation I will praise you… for [you] did not despise or abhor the affliction of the afflicted; [you] did not hide [your] face from me, but heard when I cried to [you]."[150] Psalm 30 implies that God desires the sharing of these personal stories; in verse 9, the psalmist cajoles and bargains for help, warning that if he dies, the earth will not be able to tell of God's saving faithfulness in his place. The psalmist asserts that God in fact desires each story of salvation to be told to others. Sometimes this telling takes a more sinister form; the psalmist may relate the destruction of his enemies, rather than his own salvation from destruction, as evidence of God's goodness.[151]

We see a New Testament example of such Gospel sharing in the story of the Samaritan Woman of John 4. After encountering Jesus and being changed by that experience, she goes to tell all the people of Sychar about this strange and holy incident. According to the evangelist, "many Samaritans from that city believed in [Jesus] because of the woman's testimony," while others believed once meeting Christ for themselves.[152] The Gospel account mentions nothing of music, but the sharing of her personal story of transformation makes the Samaritan Woman a model for those who use Gospel songs to tell of their salvation.[153]

---

[150] Psalm 22:22,24.

[151] See Psalm 64:7-9 as an example of this.

[152] John 4:39-42.

[153] The Samaritan woman herself features in the more recent Gospel song, "Fill My Cup, Lord:" "Like the woman at the well I was seeking for things that could not satisfy; and then I head my Savior speaking 'Draw from

99

The apostle Paul is another model of Gospel song-style sharing of personal testimony. He describes the simple approach common to this genre when he explains to the Christians at Corinth: "I did not come proclaiming the mystery of God to you in lofty words or wisdom. For I decided to know nothing among you except Jesus Christ, and him crucified."[154] Gospel song-singers of the nineteenth, twentieth, and twenty-first centuries see themselves as Paul's spiritual descendants, sharing the testimony God has given them in simple words that all can hear and understand.

Finally, Paul specifically mentions music in his first letter to the church at Corinth: "When you come together, each one has a hymn, a lesson, a revelation, a tongue, or an interpretation. Let all things be done for building up" (1 Cor 14:26). Here, the hymns that are mentioned seem to be personal statements of faith, brought by individuals in order to build up the faith of others. Such hymns seem to have been sung as solos rather than as the congregational vehicles that we now call "hymns." In Colossians 3:16, the close proximity of singing "psalms, hymns, and spiritual songs" to the need to "teach and admonish one another" hint that music could have been a way for individuals in the community to encourage one another with accounts of their own faith and understanding. These passages describes the way in which gospel songs function as testimonies, shared by individuals for the benefit of the community.

---

my well that never shall run dry.'" See *Worship and Song* (Nashville: Abingdon Press, 2011), 3093.

[154] 1 Corinthians 2:1-2.

CRITICISM OF GOSPEL SONGS

Despite this Biblical validation, Gospel songs have always been subject to harsh criticism. As mentioned earlier, hymnal editors kept the entire genre out of mainline denominational hymnals for decades after Gospel songs became popular. Now that congregations sing Gospel songs regularly in worship, the criticisms of earlier eras may not be entirely obvious. It is important to understand these criticisms, however, for they continue to arise in various forms wherever different styles or genres of worship music are discussed. We shall examine, first, complaints concerning the texts of Gospel songs, and then those concerning Gospel music.

Carlton Young includes a critique of Gospel songs in his introduction to Christian hymns *My Great Redeemer's Praise.* He finds that they ignore the earthly life, ministry, and teachings of Jesus, in direct contradiction to the four gospel accounts of Jesus' significance. He notes a lack of any indication that Christ choose or assented to the crucifixion; the Messiah is often portrayed as the Lamb sacrificed by the first person of the Trinity with no will or say in the matter. Young bemoans the copious references to "the all-sufficient blood of Jesus [which] is splashed on stanza after stanza," without an orthodox theology of sacrifice or atonement.[155] Finally, he points out that Gospel songs mention sin but never allow for the true confession of particular sins, either personal or social. The "once and for all" salvation of the Gospel song ignores the reality of the human need for continual forgiveness as we struggle with systemic and individual evils.

Other theological weaknesses lurk in Gospel songs. Many lyrics imply that once one has become a Christian, life will be an easy journey

---

[155]Young, *My Great Redeemer's Praise,* 98-99.

to heaven.[156] Only extremely rarely does the question of theodicy arise, leaving new Christians attracted by the Gospel song message without the theological wherewithal to weather difficulties or maintain faith in the face of hard questions. With their focus on the individual's experience and choice to follow Christ, Gospel songs never broach the communal nature of the Christian community (rooted in the divine "community" of the Holy Trinity, another topic frequently ignored by Gospel songs). They can, however, appear to foster a "pie in the sky" mentality that does not encourage Christians to engage with the coming of God's Kingdom in the here-and-now. Personal salvation becomes the only result that matters, and the needs of the poor, stewardship of creation, and concerns of social justice are often forgotten.

Composers of Gospel music worked to keep their tunes simple, accessible, optimistic, and appealing. Their one desire was to create music that would be popular and spread quickly. Although such attractiveness might seem to be a virtue in the service of the Gospel, church musicians have not always believed this to be true. Ralph Vaughan Williams, the editor of the 1906 *The English Hymnal*, explained his reasons for wariness in the preface to that collection.

> [M]any of the tunes of the present day which have become familiar and, probably merely from association, popular with congregations are quite unsuitable to their purpose. More often than not they are positively harmful to those who sing and hear them... The usual argument in favour of bad music is that the fine tunes are doubtless "musically correct", but that the people want "something simple". Now the expression "musically correct" has no meaning; the only "correct" music is that which is beautiful and noble. As for simplicity, what could be simpler

---

156 United Methodist scholar Ron Anderson has noted that in that denomination's hymnal, many if not most of the gospel songs are included in the section entitled "Strength in Tribulation." Although people look to Gospel songs in difficult times, whether because of their familiarity or their optimism, one could justly ask if these songs provide the most faithful and theologically sound response to tribulation.

than "St. Anne" or "The Old Hundredth", and what could be finer?[157]

It is indeed a moral rather than a musical issue. No doubt it requires a certain effort to tune oneself to the moral atmosphere implied by a fine melody; and it is far easier to dwell in the miasma of the languishing and sentimental hymn tunes which so often disfigure our services. Such poverty of heart may not be uncommon, but at least it should not be encouraged by those who direct the services of the Church; it ought no longer to be true anywhere that the most exalted moments of a church-goer's week are associated with music that would not be tolerated in any place of secular entertainment.[158]

It must be noted that Vaughan Williams rants not against the Gospel tunes of the American nineteenth-century but concerning the English Victorian hymn tunes of the same age: melodies and harmonies that were not as simplistic as their American cousins, but equally sentimental. The editor of *The English Hymnal*, himself both a composer of "classical" music and an admirer of folk melodies, has no complaints against simplicity *per se*. He objects strenuously, however, to the maudlin romanticism that Victorian hymn tunes and Gospel song melodies evoke. He finds this "miasma" unsuitable to the vigor and faith of Christianity. In other words, these popular tunes create a false "moral atmosphere," and therefore can cause great harm to the congregations that use them. Again, it is not the popularity of Gospel tunes and Victorian hymns that makes them harmful; Vaughan Williams later notes that an "average congregation likes fine melody when it can get it, but it is apt to be undiscriminating, and will often take to bad melody

---

[157] The tunes for "O God, Our Help in Ages Past" and "Praise God, from Whom All Blessings Flow."

[158] Ralph Vaughan Williams, "Preface to *The English Hymnal with Tunes*," in *Hymnody: A Collection of Source Readings*, ed. David W. Music (Lanham, Maryland: Scarecrow Press, 1996), 170-171.

when good is not forthcoming."[159] It is the meaning that the music implies which he finds untruthful and therefore dangerous.

Ralph Vaughan Williams has a modern counterpart in Frank Burch Brown, a popular writer in the fields of aesthetics and religion. In order to get at the question of how, and what, music can mean independent of any text, Burch Brown wrote a metrical version of Psalm 23 that fits the melody of "Rudolph the Red-Nosed Reindeer." To his surprise, the author has found a growing number of people who find such a musical setting charming and appropriate, despite its one-sided cheerfulness. As Burch Brown describes it, "this is prancing and dancing music, with scarcely a cloud in its melodic and harmonic sky...[it] extinguishes any sobering thoughts that might arise when walking through valleys as dark as death... [and] has us imagine a pleasant valley detour that is little more than a lark."[160] Because it lies about the truth of the Psalm, the author finds this tune inappropriate. Yet he notes a move in Christian culture toward "casual levity" and "happy optimism," a mindset which "requires just two things [of church music]: (1) that the music have scriptural or Christian words; and (2) that the music be immediately appealing."[161] Such a description seems to fit the Gospel song genre to a tee, and it reminds us that Burch Brown and Vaughan Williams have good reason to call us to consider other criteria than attractiveness and familiarity. It can be challenging to think about what melody, harmony, and rhythm imply, independent of the texts they

---

[159] Ibid., 171.

[160] Frank Burch Brown, "Christian Music: More than Just the Words," in *Inclusive Yet Discerning: Navigating Worship Artfully* (Grand Rapids: Eerdmans, 2009) 92.

[161] Ibid., 97. Alternative ways of evaluating music for worship, suggested by Burch Brown, include attending to the "fitting[ness] to a given religious purpose" of each melody or composition.

accompany, but this is a challenge that leaders and musicians in the Church must take up.

INTRODUCING THIS FUNCTION INTO THE WORSHIP OF OTHER TRADITIONS

Despite these cautions, many congregations may want to include the practices of testimony and emotional openness that the Gospel song fosters. For some congregations, the simplicity of these songs may provide a needed complement to different styles of music that are more complicated. For others, the emotional texts of the Gospel song might bring useful contrast to the more didactic or theologically complex texts of their usual music fare. In any case, there are ways for congregations to "test the waters" of the Gospel style.

A first step might include making room in worship for solo performances. Since the Gospel song is primarily an individual's witness to how God has acted in his or her life, congregations need to be willing to listen to solo music as they would listen to a prayer request, a scripture lesson, or a sermon offered by an individual. It is all too easy for congregation members to slip into a passive attitude when listening to music in worship. When experiencing music passively, the congregation listens in order to enjoy the sounds of the music and the hard work of the performer. Yet worshipping calls for a more active form of listening. Congregations that attempt such active listening attend to the meaning and significance of the words. They search for ways in which the Spirit may move through the music. They attune themselves to the "moral atmosphere" of the piece, and contemplate how God might speak to them through this aural experience. They seek understanding rather than enjoyment through their listening.

Worship leaders who wish to incorporate some Gospel sensibilities into their worship must, therefore, prepare soloists to offer their contributions as personal witnesses to the movement of God in their lives, rather than as merely musical components to beautify the worship service. And they must prepare the congregation to listen to the soloist in an active and participatory way, seeking together with the soloist how God has been and may be present. Leaders could encourage their congregations to receive such sung testimony just as they would a spoken testimony of faith.

The ethos of the Gospel song is one that values individual experience. Some congregations may be hesitant about including this personal testimony alongside such universal and timeless elements of worship as scripture readings, the Lord's Prayer, creeds, and other components. Yet this push into personal territory may be beneficial for congregations that need to see God acting in the present just as God has acted in the past. Music can be perceived as a safe way of introducing emotion and individual testimony into worship. Congregations often sing what they dare not say. Music can safely unbind the cultural stigma attached to the free expression of feelings. Therefore, worship leaders who want to encourage their congregations to allow more emotion into their worship might justifiably turn to Gospel songs.

Familiar Gospel songs such as "Blessed Assurance" and "Leaning on the Everlasting Arms" could be not only sung but also discussed. Leaders could mine these and other texts for the vision they share of a God who "whispers of love" to us, who encircles Christians with "blessed peace" in a divine embrace. Although Gospel songs do not provide a complete theological understanding of our relationship to the Creator, they can provide a corrective to those unused to understanding God's power and love at a personal level.

As much as Gospel songs have influenced Christian worship through their use as an attractive musical vehicle for personal testimony, they have also helped to create the praise and worship genre, an incredibly powerful force in the worship of Christian churches around the globe. The next chapter will investigate how these new descendants of the Gospel song unleash praise in many congregations.

CHAPTER 5: SINGING IN THE CONTEMPORARY WORSHIP MUSIC TRADITION
SONG AS PRAISE

It was a whole new deal to teach our people to emote and express their love for God freely as well. Most of us had spent a lifetime singing songs without engaging our hearts and our souls in what we were doing. None of us had ever raised out heads, our hands, or our hearts.[162]

This isn't music to appreciate; it's music to experience.[163]

Terminology may be more slippery, or subtle, in this chapter than in any other. The music of this style is alternately called praise and worship (or, more briefly, P&W), contemporary, contemporary Christian music (or CCM), contemporary worship music (or CWM), rock, pop, worship songs, choruses, and praise music, not to mention critics' more snide labels such as "seven-eleven" songs.[164] For the purpose of this study, we will follow the lead of Robert Woods and Brian Walrath and adopt the inclusive term "contemporary worship music." This phrase distinguishes between Christian songs heard on the radio but not used in church from those intended for and used in worship. It also makes room for a variety of music styles, from rock to pop and from folk to screamo.

---

[162] Joe Horness, "Contemporary Music-Driven Worship" in *Exploring the Worship Spectrum*, ed. Paul Basden (Grand Rapids: Zondervan, 2004,) 108.

[163] Andrew Beaujon, *Body Piercing Saved My Life: Inside the Phenomenon of Christian Rock* (Cambridge, Massachusetts: Da Capo, 2006), 159.

[164] Songs with seven words, repeated eleven times. This disparaging nickname is meant to mock the repetitive character of many contemporary worship music songs.

History of Contemporary Worship Music

CWM coalesced as the result of several influences in worship, music, and culture, both within and outside of the Church. Robb Redman identifies three of these influences in his book *The Great Worship Awakening*: the praise and worship movement, the contemporary worship music industry, and the seeker service.[165]

Redman identifies the charismatic strain of emotionalism, and the music that serves as a vehicle for this, as the "praise and worship movement." He finds antecedents for this approach in the "soul-stirring hymns" of Charles Wesley, the frontier worship of camp meetings and revivals, and the "spiritual intensity and emotional and physical expression" of early Pentecostal worship. Redman identifies the Latter Rain movement, a Pentecostal renewal of the 1940's and 1950's, as the source of "short worship songs, known as scripture songs or praise choruses" – a direct ancestor of CWM.[166] Each of these musical predecessors to modern CWM emphasized the importance of emotional intensity in relating to God. These styles of music represent a theological position that views experience as a testimony of salvation,

---

[165] Robb Redman, *The Great Worship Awakening: Singing a New Song in the Postmodern Church* (San Francisco: Jossey-Bass, 2002). Redman actually identifies four movements that he believes influence not only contemporary worship but the future worship of the "postmodern church." Three of his streams of influence seem to lead directly to CWM, while the fourth, the liturgical renewal movement, has remained outside of the interest or influence of contemporary worship. I will therefore present Redman's surveys of seeker services, the praise and worship movement, and the CWM industry without tying these phenomena to postmodernism or Ancient-Future worship (to which they relate far less directly), but seeing them as factors in contemporary worship. As musicians and congregations that have adopted CWM seem unaffected by the liturgical renewal movement, I will not address that topic in this chapter.

[166] Ibid., 31.

and therefore a blessing greatly to be desired. We see this experiential emphasis in the passionate language of Charles Wesley's hymns (who referred to Jesus as "lover of my soul," and begged to "let me to [Jesus'] bosom fly," for example) as well as in the intimate texts of adoration that make up many praise choruses. [167] Of course, these characteristics featured in the Gospel Songs explored in the previous chapter, and they are also related to the charismatic songs to be studied in the next chapter. But it is in combination with several other movements and forces, described below, that the praise and worship movement contributed to the formation of CWM.

In his chapter on the contemporary worship music industry, Redman points out the enormous influence that both Christian and secular "songwriters, artists, producers, publishers, and distributors" have had on what Christians sing in worship.[168] This industry began with the music publishing of popular revival Gospel musicians such as Ira Sankey and Homer Rodeheaver, who worked with preachers Dwight Moody and Billy Sunday. These publishers mixed their religious desire for evangelism with a business concern for making profits. Music publishers following World War II focused on the youth market, creating Christian music that reflected the secular music tastes of their young audience. The Jesus Music of the 1960's and 1970's further solidified the bond between the sounds of rock music and the message of

---

[167] While Wesley's hymns were indeed marked by emotional intensity and passionate phrases, they were also strongly informed by his thorough knowledge of the Bible, his readings of early Church Fathers and Orthodox as well as Protestant theologians, and his desire to link singing to the church year, the celebration of the sacraments, and other hallmarks of worship in the Church of England. These latter traits account for distinction between the corpus of Wesley's hymns and much of CWM.

[168] Ibid., 48.

Christianity. Redman names the four major Christian music companies that continued this work when he wrote: Maranatha! Music, the Vineyard Music Group, Integrity Music, and Worship Together.[169] Now, almost fifteen years after the publication of Redman's work, the music industry continues to change. Each of the four companies that Redman discussed continue to issue new music, but the rise of internet technology and ways to share and spread music has allowed singer-songwriters to make an entry into the market without signing with a major label. Denominational publishing houses have also sought ways to participate in the work, and the profits, of the music industry.

In addition to these changes in the sound of music for worship, its sources of production, and its emotional ethos, Redman notes the attention musicians and worship leaders have paid to evangelism. He sees the roots of this seeker focus in the outdoor preaching of George Whitefield and John Wesley, the frontier camp meetings of the nineteenth century, the urban revivals of the Gospel song era, and the popular preaching of Sister Aimee McPherson and Robert Schuller. This evangelistic focus blossomed in modern-day churches such as Willow Creek, where worship is created explicitly for those who are not yet Christians. Redman also sees a connection between these seeker services and the church growth movement, which uses "the social sciences of sociology, ethnography, and demographics to understand how people live, think, and feel."[170]

Redman brings up the crucial influence of the media on worship that uses CWM. Evangelists have always used whatever tools they could to spread their message of the gospel. The radio, and its surrounding

---

[169] Ibid., 55.

[170] Ibid., 12.

111

culture of music publishers, recording companies, and constantly changing top-ten lists, affected the way music is spread and understood within CWM. Prior to this movement, church music was available through hymnals and songbooks, either denominationally produced or (more rarely) tied to particular composers. Congregations sang exclusively from the collections that their congregations owned. Collections were assembled from selections appropriate (in the minds of the editors) to Sunday morning worship or to evening prayer meetings or gospel sings. These hymnals and songbooks lasted for decades, often, and so the repertoire of a congregation changed only slowly.

With the adoption of the industry model of music creation and propagation, congregations now first encounter new music through radio contact or social media, rather than through the pages of a hymnal. Likewise, the "experts" in charge of identifying appropriate music for worship have become music industry executives rather than the pastors, church musicians, and denominational leaders who assemble hymnals. The industry determines the amount of radio play for each new song, and therefore the likelihood of congregational adoption of new music. As with secular radio, songs are created to immediately attract an audience and then to be quickly replaced by something newer. With such a disposable style of music, hymnals (which take years to produce and may be expected to last decades) can no longer serve congregations' ever-changing repertoire. The company Christian Copyright Licensing International arose to provide copyright permission to churches using CWM, so that congregations could change their musical choices "spontaneously."[171] Yet the theological implications of using such a

---

[171] www.ccli.com/WhoWeAre/ accessed June 21, 2010. The word "spontaneous", used by CCLI, is rather misleading, since congregations using CCLI must print or project a short copyright statement after each song used. This takes some advance preparation. However, the use of this word demonstrates the self-understanding of CWM users that this

disposable medium to convey an eternal message seem rarely to be addressed. Likewise, the notion of choosing a congregation as one might choose a radio station – in order to hear favorites rather than receive exposure to new or challenging messages or sounds – needs to be explored further.

In addition to radio, television has greatly affected worship in churches using CWM. Television evangelists created the expectation for professional-looking settings in which to engage in worship. Through television broadcasting, people in even the smallest and poorest communities could see expensive and attractive attire, architecture, and furnishings. The expectations for what worship should look like changed. Basilica-style church buildings with generations-old pews and props looked suddenly shabby beside the sets of the television evangelists. Viewers compared not only quality but also style. Worship leaders began to borrow design ideas from talk show hosts. The altar, cross, and pulpit ceded ground to potted plants, a stage for the band, and portable microphones for preachers. New media forms, including social networking venues and recording and broadcasting technologies, continue to provide tools for the worship of CWM congregations, even as they also shape that worship.

---

music, and this way of using music, allows for more freedom and expression than does the use of music from a hymnal or other printed collection. The use of the screen, however, removes from the congregation any chance to choose its own music. When congregants hold hymnals, they may suggest hymns to be sung, truly "spontaneous" requests that music leaders can solicit during hymn sings or at other times in worship. Without hymnals, congregations do not have in their possession a list of the music available, much less copies of every song. Just as other forms of technology (radio, television, internet) have affected worship in many congregations, the use of projection continues to affect how congregations are able to use music in worship.

For a musical form that is often called "praise and worship," it is unsurprising that the purpose of such music is overwhelmingly the praise of God. The bulk of CWM songs in most worship services are sung at the beginning of the gathering, in order to draw the congregation's attention to God and offer up praise. This act of praise, often made up of four or five or even more songs, serves as a preliminary activity to the hearing of the Word, read from scripture and preached in sermon.[172] Moreover, this praise can be expressed in several different ways.

CCLI, mentioned above, keeps lists of their twenty-five most-requested songs over six month periods. A survey of the top songs from April through September of 2009 illuminates the ways in which various facets of praising God appear in this genre.[173]

The theme of God's power and worthiness to be praised occurs frequently among the songs: seventeen of the top twenty-five titles focus on this aspect of praise. Song lyrics lift up God's intrinsic majesty, naming the Creator "Lord of all creation, of the water, earth, and sky... God of wonders beyond our galaxy" or "Our hope, our Strong Deliverer...

---

[172] While CWM can serve to prepare congregations to be receptive to the Word, preached later in the service, the close thematic connection between scripture passages and hymns, discussed in chapter 3, does not obtain here. While there may be some link between the preacher's main topic and the lyrics of a song or songs from the opening set, such a connection is not considered essential in this style.

[173] This list was the most recent option available at the initial writing of this chapter. In this list, one of the songs was a version of John Newton's hymn "Amazing Grace." Since that text is not a true representative of the CWM genre, I excluded it from my survey.

the everlasting God."[174] Sometimes these ascriptions draw on scriptural imagery, as this text inspired by the book of Revelation: "Clothed in rainbows of living color, flashes of lightning, rolls of thunder,/ blessing and honor, strength and glory and power be to you, the only Wise King."[175] Other songs locate God's worthiness in the divine ability to respond to human weakness, declaring that God is "mighty to save... Author of salvation."[176]

Yet another sub-theme occurs just as frequently. Seventeen of the top twenty-five songs describe the worshipper him- or herself, delving into the act, feelings, and even posture of worshipping itself. Singers of CWM lyrics narrate their praise. Such self-reflective singing can be communal: "we're singing for the glory of the risen King," "we stand and lift up our hands... we bow down and worship him now," "we welcome you here Lord Jesus."[177] More frequently, however, it is individual: "my heart will sing," "I sing for joy," "It's my joy to honor you," "Lord I love to sing your praises."[178] Songs dwell on the physical manifestations of worship, describing hands raised, bodies standing, backs bent in bowing, and laying metaphorical crowns before the feet of Jesus. Lyrics also highlight the pleasurable aspects of worship,

---

[174] Lyrics from "God of Wonders" by Marc Byrd and Steve Hindalong and ""Everlasting God" by Brenton Brown and Ken Riley.

[175] Lyrics from "Revelation Song" by Jennie Lee Riddle.

[176] Lyrics from "Mighty to Save" by Ben Fielding and Morgan Reuben.

[177] Lyrics from "Mighty to Save," "Holy is the Lord" by Chris Tomlin and Louie Giglio, and "Hosanna (Praise is Rising)" by Paul Baloche and Brenton Brown.

[178] Lyrics from "How Great is our God" by Chris Tomlin, Jesse Reeves, and Ed Cash, ""Shout to the Lord," by Darlene Zschech, ""You are my King," by Billy Foote, and "Lord I Lift your Name on High" by Rick Founds.

reinforcing the congregation's willingness to participate. As Joel Houston wrote in "From the Inside Out," "my purpose remains the art of losing myself in bringing you praise." That experience of "losing oneself" in a crowd of worshippers and a wave of sound fascinates and attracts both worshippers and songwriters. Many are wary of this attraction. Matt Redman wrote "The Heart of Worship" in response to the idolatry that CWM can inspire:

> Verse 1: When the music fades
> and all is stripped away
> and I simply come,
> longing just to bring
> something that's of worth,
> that will bless your heart.
>
> Bridge: I'll bring you more than a song,
> for a song in itself
> is not what you have required.
> You search much deeper within,
> through the way things appear.
> You're looking into my heart.
>
> Chorus: I'm coming back to the heart of worship,
> and it's all about you, all about you, Jesus.
> I'm sorry, Lord, for the thing I've made it.
> when it's all about you, it's all about you, Jesus.[179]

The song continues, with one more verse and several repetitions of the bridge and chorus. Even in Redman's desire to confess that he has preferred the worship music to the God worshipped, he cannot completely avoid fixating, yet again, on the experience of worshipping. The chorus is telling; although worship is "all about you, Jesus," the subject is "I." The song narrates the worshipper's experience and feelings: "I simply come... I'll bring you more than a song... I'm

---

[179] Matt Redman, © 1999 Thankyou Music (Admin. by Capitol CMG Publishing) Used by permission.

coming back... I'm sorry..." The function of praising with CWM, then, is a complex one. As frequently as songs center on God who is worthy of praise, they also center on those who are doing the praising.

Secondary aspects of praising, as it occurs in CWM, are Christ's resurrection, human frailty and need, and a desire to call others to worship. Eight of the songs refer explicitly to the suffering, death, and resurrection of Jesus as a reason for praise. Six songs include descriptions of human need and sin – factors which may inhibit praise but which have been answered and covered by God's mercy and Christ's sacrifice, therefore making explicit the worthiness of God to be praised. Finally, four songs serve as calls to worship, summoning all those within hearing distance to join in the praise.

THE AMPLIFYING ROLE OF CONTEMPORARY WORSHIP MUSIC

If the texts of CWM songs function as calls to praise, reminders of reasons to praise, and mirrors of the act of praising, the music functions as an emotional intensifier of this activity. Authors struggle to identify this role as they describe what the sound of rock music does, but they continually hint in this direction. Herbert London believes that rock music "weaves emotion around events and human relationships," creates a "world of feelings and senses," and "move[s] listeners."[180] Doug Van Pelt, creator and editor of *HM Magazine* (a publication for fans of Christian metal music), explains "rock 'n' roll epitomizes parts of humanity. Wonderful parts, you know, passion, emotion, angst, and

---

[180] Herbert I. London, *Closing the Circle: A Cultural History of the Rock Revolution* (Chicago: Nelson-Hall, 1984), 21-23.

117

even aggression and anger that can be channeled in positive ways."[181] When asked what he looks for in Christian music, he answers "emotional impact, something I could identify with. A common emotion... there's [sic] certain areas emotionally that music can touch."[182]

According to pediatrician and scholar Victor C. Strasburger, young people profess to like rock music for its ability to regulate their moods and emotions.[183]

Brad Herring, author of a manual on using technology in worship, locates much of the emotion-building ability of CWM music in its lower frequencies. He writes that a key method "to build excitement and energy in a room is to 'pump up the bass...' In contemporary services, a significant enabler of excitement in a mix is a quality subwoofer."[184]

Scientists, too, have probed rock music for its attraction to listeners. In a 1999 study, psychologist Neil P. McAngus Todd and biologist Frederick W. Cody attempted to discern the way in which such loud music creates pleasure rather than the stress associated with equally loud industrial noise. They believe that rock music over a certain decibel level creates a pleasurable response in the vestibular system of the human ear, a response similar to that "obtained from

[181] Andrew Beaujon, *Body Piercing Saved My Life: Inside the Phenomenon of Christian Rock* (Cambridge, Massachusetts: D Capo Press, 2006), 50.

[182] Ibid., 54.

[183] Victor C. Strasburger, *Adolescents and the Media: Medical and Psychological Impact* (Thousand Oaks, California: SAGE Publications, 1995), 82.

[184] Brad Herring, *Sound, Lighting, and Video: A Resource for Worship* (New York: Focal Press, 2009), 22-23.

swings, rocking chairs, and fun parks, for example."[185] Listeners, or worshippers, thus experience loud rock music as physically pleasurable in a way that quieter music cannot match.

In some ways, this music furthers the goals of the texts of many CWM songs. If the purpose of praise songs is to foster the worship and adoration of God, then the congregation must want to enter into this praise. Lyrically, CWM songs encourage this activity by reminding singers of God's greatness and worthiness and of the pleasure of entering into worship. In other words, they strive to make the congregation members *feel* like praising God. Rock music, with its sonic intensity and pleasurable vestibular reactions, strengthens those feelings. The music acts as an amplifier, expanding emotions and impressions. With help from the aural atmosphere of the music, God's greatness becomes overwhelming and the joys of worship become intoxicating. As Andrew Beaujon affirmed in the quotation at the beginning of this chapter, CWM is deeply experiential, both emotionally and physically. One does not appreciate CWM from the outside but becomes engulfed by its sensory world and experiences it from the inside.

Church leaders who foster CWM probably have other functions entirely in mind when they choose this style of music for their congregations. Most pastors or worship leaders articulate a desire to use the "music of the people" in employing rock music. This echoes the function of Gospel music in aligning the sounds of the church and the sounds of the secular world, thus making the message of these songs

---

[185] Neil P. McAngus Todd and Frederick W. Cody, "Vestibular responses to loud dance music: A physiological basis of the 'rock and roll threshold'?" *Journal of the Acoustical Society of America* 107 (January 2000): 499. The vestibular system affects balance and orientation.

more palatable. Yet this is only a secondary byproduct of the function of Christian rock music used in worship, for two reasons.

First, whether or not church leaders, pastors, or even church musicians themselves are aware of the ability of rock music to coalesce and enhance emotion in no way limits its capacity to do so. Church leaders may be aware that such music is popular and effective, but they may not be able to articulate the sonic root of its popularity. While they opt to employ CWM because it is well-liked, particularly among younger Christian congregations, the emotional amplification inherent in this musical form lies behind its popularity.

Secondly, critics, musicians, and Christian audiences alike have long questioned to what extent CWM actually sounds like secular rock. In a 1995 survey of 479 teenagers about music in worship, those respondents who did not typically attend church disapproved of CWM selections. According to the creator of this survey, many of the unchurched teenagers "wrote on their survey forms: 'This sounds like my parents' music!'" She concluded that "the unchurched teenagers were apparently influenced by the standards of popular culture, which would judge the sound of most contemporary Christian music to be neither contemporary nor popular."[186]

SCRIPTURAL UNDERSTANDING OF EMOTIONAL PRAISE

The concept of worship music as praise or thanksgiving is a strongly biblical one. As Calvin Stapert finds in his survey of early Christian thought about music,

---

[186] www.lcms.org/pages/internal.asp?NavID=708 accessed June 23, 2010.

The New Testament begins and ends with outbursts of song. The birth of Jesus brought about the first outburst – four songs recorded in the first two chapters of Luke. Mary sang the *Magnificat* (1:46-55), Zechariah the *Benedictus* (1:68-79), Simeon the *Nunc dimittis* (2:29-32), and the angels sang "Glory to God in the highest, and on earth peace among those with whom he is pleased" (2:14). The second outburst occurs in Revelation: there the song to the Lamb is picked up in ever-widening circles until the whole cosmos joins in.[187]

The early Church, according to Stapert, continued to value the doxological function of music in worship as a vital role.

Even beyond words of praise, the writers, performers, and fans of CWM have prized the emotional abandon fostered by the sounds of rock music. They explain and justify such radical, almost reckless, openness by pointing to the story of King David in 2 Samuel 6. In the scriptural account, David brings the ark of the covenant to Jerusalem, "leaping and dancing" in a less-than-dignified way. David's wife, Michal, mocks her husband for his lack of dignity, and he responds "I will make myself yet more contemptible than this." The fact that his dancing was dedicated to God is viewed as important, while the cultural ideas of appropriateness which trouble Michal are seen as trivial.

The way in which this passage reflects the identity of CWM is seen in its presence in the 1995 song "Undignified" by Matt Redman:

> I will dance, I will sing
> To be mad for my King
> Nothing, Lord, is hindering
> This passion in my soul
> And I'll become
> Even more undignified than this

---

187 Calvin R. Stapert, *A New Song for an Old World: Musical Thought in the Early Church* (Grand Rapids: Eerdmans, 2007), 14.

Some may say it's foolishness
But I'll become
Even more undignified than this
Leave my pride by my side
Etc[188]

A recent CCLI search revealed seven more songs with the word "undignified" in the title, revealing a strong proclivity to following in David's abandoned footsteps.

Another Biblical basis for understanding CWM is found in the Colossians/Ephesians passage mentioned in previous chapters. In each pericope, Paul mentions that music-making should be done "in your hearts." Since the heart has, in Western European culture, been traditionally understood as the locus for emotion, this passage can be viewed by CWM advocates as an affirmation of the emotional nature of this musical expression.

CWM practitioners often contrast their heart-felt and emotionally saturated singing and worship with the more intellectual and drier styles found in other traditions. They interpret this contrast through the prophets' mandate to avoid empty words and rituals in the worship of God. Joe Horness points his readers to Isaiah 29:13 when offering an apology of contemporary worship practices: "The Lord said: because these people draw near with their mouths and honor me with their lips, while their hearts are far from me, and their worship of me is a human commandment learned by rote; so I will again do amazing things with this people, shocking and amazing." Musicians and worship leaders who support CWM may see that movement as both an antidote for the "human commandment learned by rote" and as one result of that

---

[188] Matt Redman, © 1995, (Admin. by Capitol CMG Publishing) Used by permission.

122

problem – as part of the "shocking and amazing" things that God is doing to break open dry worship and distant hearts.[189]

CRITICISM OF CONTEMPORARY WORSHIP MUSIC

The critiques of CWM are many and familiar. The most foundational criticism is that rock music, no matter what the lyrical content, is inappropriate for Christian worship. Some claim that this music is physically destructive: the very rhythms and musical patterns of rock damage the body and the mind.[190] Others fear that the sounds of rock are morally pernicious, citing a story of an American missionary told by African natives that rock music uses "the very beats ... once used to conjure up evil spirits in their pagan dances."[191] This claim assumes that since rock rhythms were once associated with evil, they can never be freed from such purposes, even among those who are unaware of previous function.

Another musical line of critique posits that rock music is fine as a vehicle for worship, but that CWM is a mediocre and unworthy

---

[189] See Horness, 100. While passages such as Isaiah 29:13 show God's dissatisfaction with "human commandments learned by rote," they also contrast the people's dutiful (if dry) worship to their unfaithful living. Horness uses this passage to indicate that God wants heart-felt, passionate worship. The scriptures indicate that God wants people's lives to echo their worship – that faithful worship should also be evident in faithful living. The connection between worship and justice is a growing concern of CMW artists (see Rend Collective's "Build Your Kingdom Here" of 2012 as an example).

[190] Mark Joseph, *The Rock & Roll Rebellion* (Nashville: Broadman and Holman, 1999), 3. Joseph cites David Noebel, who claims that rock music causes damage to muscles, adrenal glands, and house plants, among other things.

[191] Ibid., 2.

substitute for real rock. Christian rock music is derided as simple, repetitive, and the result of imitation rather than true inspiration. This complaint, referred to earlier, also serves as a call to CWM musicians to strengthen the quality of their art. That call is voiced strongly by Doug Van Pelt, editor and publisher of *HM*, a Christian hard rock magazine. Van Pelt writes:

> Ever seen a tall kid in a basketball game with a bunch of smaller kids? If he's got any talent, he'll dominate. In the same way, an artist with a little bit of talent is going to get noticed a lot quicker if the competition he or she is facing is not quite as talented. If not developed properly, that artist will get put into the system of recording and performing before he or she is really ready. This produces inferior art that the Christian public is asked to accept as "the Christian counterpart to that evil and corrupt secular stuff." While the "secular" artist may be promoting sin with his or her lifestyle and integrating anti-biblical attitudes and thought into its [sic] music, at least that artist is having to develop its [sic] craft in a more competitive atmosphere where excellence is the standard.[192]

Several other complaints address the texts and theology of CWM songs. The overabundance of the personal pronoun in the genre is so well known that in a study of "male perception of romantic lyrics in contemporary worship music," the interview subjects expressed more disapproval of the subjective "I, me, and my" nature of many CWM songs than they did of the metaphor of Jesus or God as boyfriend or lover.[193] Critics believe, not without cause in some instances, that CWM centers

---

[192] Doug Van Pelt, "The Ugly Truth Behind Christian Rock," *HM: The Hard Music Magazine* 104 (November/December 2003): 38.

[193] Keith Drury, "I'm Desperate for You: Male Perception of Romantic Lyrics in Contemporary Worship Music," in *The Message and the Music,* ed. Robert Woods and Brian Walrath (Nashville: Abingdon Press, 2007), 60.

on the individual and his or her emotions and desires rather than on God.

The study mentioned above suggests another weakness in many CWM songs. Jenell Williams Paris has written convincingly about the way in which contemporary American culture has reduced the Biblical understanding of love to fit modern romantic notions about love. With that cultural understanding in place, the God of the praise songs becomes a romantic hero who protects and rescues the individual. Songs that veer in this direction have been dismissed as "Jesus is my boyfriend" songs, yet they make up a large percentage of current CWM favorites.[194]

Others find a lack of orthodox Christian understanding in CWM lyrics, or even the presence of heretical ideas. In a recent honors research project at Northwestern College, student Andrew Klumpp found that the vast majority of songs used on campus in worship during contemporary services referred to a nebulous God, neither Trinitarian nor discernibly one of the three persons of the Trinity. Some songs have so few lines of poetry, repeated so many times, that a three- or four-minutes song may be bereft of any theological description of God. Or lyricists may include references or direct quotations of Biblical verses, but they may not explain these images enough to make theological sense in the course of the song.[195]

---

[194] Jenell Williams Paris, "I Could Sing of Your Love Forever: American Romance in Contemporary Worship Music," in *The Message and the Music*, 46.

[195] Nick Page writes, "The Dadaist poets used to practice random poetry; they would cut up a book into separate words or sentences, throw them in the air and paste them together how they landed. Sometimes I suspect that many worship song writers use a similar approach. Throw a load of scripture verses in the air, let them land and then just glue them together. It's fridge-magnet poetry; not really lyric-writing, just rearranging verses to fit." *And Now Let's Move into a Time of Nonsense:*

A further complaint concerning CWM targets neither the music not the texts of songs, but the manner of presenting them. Most congregations using CWM project the words to a song on a screen or screens, but do not include the melodies. Those who are unfamiliar with the songs have no way to sing along, and are therefore identified as "outsiders."

Another issue which may hamper congregational participation is that of the soloistic nature of many CWM songs. As Bert Polman explains:

> When [Praise & Worship] music began to appear, it was marketed as congregational music, even though much of it was composed by CCM artists whose primary experience was with small ensembles, not with congregations. These artists were accustomed to rehearsing music prior to performance and would work out the interpretation of complex rhythmic patterns and extended formal structures with their soloists and small teams of instrumentalists.[196]

It should be noted that as familiar as these criticisms are, they are often inaccurate. Like all forms of music, CWM has changed and grown since its beginnings in the 1960's and 1970's. Current songwriters often bring keen musical sensibilities and wise theological perspectives to their craft. There are many examples of CWM songs that avoid painting God into a narrow "knight in shining armor" role, or keep a communal rather than an individual point of view. One can also find CWM songs that make clear distinctions between the persons of the

---

Why Worship Songs are Failing the Church (Waynesboro, Georgia: Authentic: 2004), 89.

[196] Bert Polman, "Praise the Name of Jesus: Are All Praise and Worship Songs for the Congregation?" in *The Message and the Music,* ed. Robert Woods and Brian Walrath (Nashville: Abingdon Press, 2007), 128.

Trinity in an orthodox yet compelling way. In Polman's study of the congregational applicability of many CWM songs, he found that nearly two-thirds of them contained appropriate ranges, rhythms, and formal structures for congregational singing.[197] Thus, while some of the above criticisms are true some of the time, there is a large corpus of musically interesting, communally appropriate, and theologically orthodox material within the CWM canon.

INTRODUCING THIS FUNCTION INTO THE WORSHIP OF OTHER TRADITIONS

Despite these criticisms, from those who participate in CWM as well as those who do not, this genre of worship music is growing in popularity. Many congregations may feel that its emphasis on emotional engagement in the praise of God would be of benefit to their worshipping practices. Such churches might try to incorporate some CWM repertoire and sensibility into their weekly worship.

One way to begin this is for the church musicians and worship leaders to think about selecting musical material in a new way. Instead of finding hymns or songs that can respond to the scripture reading(s) or sermon topic, leaders can identify songs that use straightforward language and emotional honesty in the praise of God. Intentionally placing such songs at the beginning of the worship service, and verbally reinforcing both the importance and the enjoyment of praise, can help the congregation to focus on a new facet of music making in church. A congregation that uses CWM will typically place several pieces of music back-to-back in order to give the congregation time to relax into an open

---

[197] Ibid., 134.

and sincere experience of worshipping God through singing praise. Without introducing any new songs or instruments, church musicians and pastors can begin to appropriate a CWM sensibility through the steps described above.

Another lesson from the CWM tradition is that of the importance of volume. As noted in the Todd and Cody study, rock music is often associated with a pleasurable sensation produced by the vestibular system of the human ear. They discerned this effect, however, only with music of 90 dB or more.[198] Congregations interested in taking advantage of this effect might consider ways to incorporate louder music from time to time. Although the amplified instruments of a typical praise team serve this purpose well, other instruments can provide an intense auditory experience, including trumpets and other brass instruments, percussion instruments including the timpani, and the organ, when played using many stops. Music leaders may discern appropriate occasions for full-throated praise of God: times when the decibel level might rise in service to the worship service.

Certainly, many congregations find the introduction of these things to be desirable. And countless authors have written books and articles on the most successful ways to include praise songs and guitars for the first time into worship with congregations unaccustomed to these things. Yet Contemporary Worship Music is more than a particular instrumentation. What gives CWM much of its appeal is its unadorned expression of praise to God, set to music of great vitality. Churches interested in bringing elements of this music into worship

---

[198] Todd and Cody, 498. Music and worship leaders from all styles of worship, however, should beware of noise-induced hearing loss, which can occur at decibel levels over 85 dB. The health and hearing of congregation members and church musicians should not be endangered during worship.

must pay attention to the emotional intensity of the style as much as its characteristic sounds.

As much attention as CWM has gained over the last years, other and quieter forms of worship have also grown in appeal to Christians. In the next chapter, we turn from music as amplified praise to music as spiritual discipline within two very different communities.

Chapter 6: Singing in the Taizé and Charismatic Traditions
Song as Spiritual Discipline

> These songs also sustain personal prayer. Through them, little
> by little, our being finds an inner unity with God. They can
> continue in the silence of our hearts while we are at work,
> speaking with others or resting. In this way prayer and daily
> life are united. They allow us to keep on praying even when we
> are unaware of it, in the silence of our hearts.[199]

> A close examination of the Bible reveals that singing is not only
> an offering of praise for what God has done in our lives, but an
> instrument for contributing to an immense spiritual
> breakthrough. Miracles and powerful works can ride on the
> wings of a song.[200]

This chapter explores what appear to be two exceedingly
different styles of music, from two separate traditions. We might
associate the music of the charismatic movement with boisterous
activity and loud shouts, exactly the opposite of what we expect from the
meditative tradition of Taizé. Yet both traditions make use of a similar
spiritual approach to music, and there is much in common between the
short chants of Taizé and the simple heart songs of the charismatics.

---

[199] www.taize.fr/en_article338.html accessed June 25, 2010.

[200] Jack W. Hayford, "Charismatic Worship: Embracing a Worship Renewal," in
Experience God in Worship by Michael D. Warden (Loveland, Colorado:
Group Publishing, 2000), 149.

THE HISTORY OF CHARISMATIC MUSIC

The Pentecostal and Charismatic movements have a history tied at every step to the worship experiences of their members. One of the more striking traits of Pentecostal worship, speaking or singing in tongues, appeared early in 1901 at a worship service among the students and supporters of Charles Parham's Bible School in Topeka, Kansas.[201] William J. Seymour, an African-American follower of Parham, brought that experience to Los Angeles in founding the Azuza Street revival a few years later.[202] While noted for its multiracial congregation and use of piano, guitar, drums, and other instruments in worship, the Azuza revival also featured a "new song:" singing either without words or in tongues that erupted in worship as a gift of the Spirit, sometimes sung by an individual and sometimes by the entire congregation at once.[203] Worship included other distinctive practices such as speaking in tongues (in addition to the singing in tongues described above) and spontaneous vocal and physical participation among members of the congregation. Marked by these features, Pentecostalism spread to Norway, England, and elsewhere as international visitors to Azuza

---

[201] Charles F. Parham, "The Latter Rain," in *Pentecostal and Charismatic Studies: A Reader*, ed. William K. Kay and Anne E. Dyer (London: SCM Press, 2004), 10-13.

[202] A visitor to Azuza who received the gift of tongues described it thus: "finally my throat began to enlarge and I felt my vocal organs being, as it were, drawn into a different shape. O, how strange and wonderful it all was to me and how blessed it was to be thus in the hands of God. Last of all I felt my tongue begin to move and my lips begin to produce strange sounds, which did not originate in my mind. In a few moments [God] was speaking clearly through me in other tongues..." William H. Durham, "Personal Testimony," in *Pentecostal and Charismatic Studies: A Reader*, ed. William K. Kay and Anne E. Dyer (London: SCM Press, 2004), 93.

[203] F. Bartlemann, "Azuza Street," in *Pentecostal and Charismatic Studies: A Reader*, ed. William K. Kay and Anne E. Dyer (London: SCM Press, 2004), 14-17.

Street returned to their own countries eager to share their experiences.[204]

After several decades, the Pentecostal movement had become institutionalized and lost much of its early energy. The first Pentecostal leaders and "pioneers began to find themselves boxed in by the bureaucratic and administrative machinery they had created for the running of the congregations that had been brought into existence."[205] Many within the denomination longed for the Spirit-led excitement of the turn of the century, and sought renewal for their church. That renewal came in the form of the Latter Rain of 1948, which "reasserted the need for contemporary apostles and prophets who were not answerable to constitutional committees and it recalled the importance of direct and overwhelming spiritual experience."[206] The critical importance of this immediate experience of God continued to assert itself in later developments among charismatics, as evidenced by the Charismatic movement of the 1960's and the "Third Wave" of the 1980's.

While the history related this far has shown how Pentecostals created new denominations, centered in part upon the critical importance of speaking in tongues as they understood had happened at the first Pentecost, the Charismatic movement of the 1960's focused on the multitude of spiritual gifts described in the New Testament. This movement spread to influence many other denominations, both Catholic

---

[204] Mark J. Cartledge, *Encountering the Spirit: The Charismatic Tradition* (London: Darton, Longman and Todd, 2006), 22.

[205] William K. Kay, "Introduction," in *Pentecostal and Charismatic Studies: A Reader*, ed. William K. Kay and Anne E. Dyer (London: SCM Press, 2004), xxii.

[206] *Ibid.* Kay cites Richard M. Riss's study *A Survey of Twentieth Century Revival Movements in North America* (Peabody, MA: Hendrickson, 1988) as one source for his conclusions.

and Protestant. Priests and pastors from these denominations experienced the Holy Spirit's power, manifested through speaking in tongues, prophecies, healings, or other signs. These leaders brought their charismatic encounters with the Spirit to bear on their work and worship in their own denominations.[207] During the 1960's, the Pentecostal mélange of instruments, including pianos, guitars, and percussion, and lively, participatory singing made their way into other traditions. Christians accustomed to the respectable and restrained worship patterns of the 1950's suddenly longed for the in-breaking of the Holy Spirit. "As the charismatic renewal surged, singing in tongues became its marker. Free-flowing harmonies joined with verbalized glossolalia were mixed with some English repetition of spontaneous ejaculatory prayers like 'Jesus, Jesus, Jesus,' or 'I love you, Lord.'"[208] This Spirit-infused worship movement then joined with the folk and rock sounds of the Jesus People, who used popular musical forms to evangelize and contemporize the Christian message.

A new form of charismatic activity and influence arose in the 1980's. This movement, known as the "Third Wave," resulted in the formation of new congregations and denominations. One of the most influential leaders of this movement was John Wimber, a musician who employed a pop-influenced style of worship song to encourage the congregation in intimate singing to God. He strove for music and worship that left people "convicted, converted, healed, and even delivered from evil spirits... Time was made to 'wait on the Lord' and to 'hear from God.'"[209] Wimber assumed leadership of the Vineyard

---

[207] Cartledge, 23.

[208] Don Williams, "Charismatic Worship" in *Exploring the Worship Spectrum* ed. Paul Basden (Grand Rapids: Zondervan, 2004), 140.

[209] Ibid., 143.

association of churches in 1982. Vineyard is one of the largest denominations to arise out of the Third Wave, and it influences wider Christian culture through a robust music publishing branch, Vineyard Music. Under Wimber's influence, Third Wave charismatics see "prophecy, words of knowledge, evangelism, and healing as signs of the in-breaking of the kingdom of God," while speaking in tongues holds less prominence than it did in previous "waves" of charismatic and Pentecostal activity.[210]

Affected by different "waves" of Pentecostal and charismatic activity, different denominations, and differing theological and doxological emphases, charismatic congregations employ a wide range of music for worship. Scholar Victoria Cooke identified five categories of songs sung in charismatic worship, including exuberant "songs of praise," more sentimental "songs of love and commitment," "songs of intercession" that have included, in the past, references to spiritual warfare, "songs of ministry," which encourage the worshipper to open up to an experience of God's presence, and "songs of awe and glory," which "celebrate the encounter of such transcendence in an immediate way."[211] This chapter largely focuses on the last category of songs.

THE HISTORY OF TAIZÉ CHANTS

The community of Taizé has its own history. Brother Roger Schütz-Marsauche founded the ecumenical religious community of Taizé as a center of reconciliation. Brother Roger, a Reformed Swiss pastor, had long been interested in monasticism, and he felt God calling him to

---

[210] Cartledge, 24.

[211] Ibid., 66-67.

live in solidarity with those who suffer; during the 1940's in Europe, that meant living in a tiny town called Taizé on the border of German-occupied France. Here, Roger assisted Jewish refugees fleeing Nazi brutality until he was discovered and escaped to Geneva. Following the war, he returned to Taizé and his community grew in members and in mission, sending brothers to live with the poor in Africa, Algeria, and Hell's Kitchen, as well as hosting ever-increasing numbers of spiritual pilgrims. By the 1960's, thousands of young people from diverse countries came to visit and worship with the brothers, drawn by their simple message of reconciliation.

The growing popularity of Taizé as a destination for pilgrims and retreatants led the brothers to reform their worship practices. Previously, Brother Roger led the community in prayer three times each day, singing nearly the entire liturgy in French. Music for these services came from the French metrical psalms of the *Genevan Psalter* as well as new compositions by Jesuit priest and musician Joseph Gelineau.[212] Yet such singing left non-Francophones unable to participate, a situation at odds with the community's inclusive spirit. Searching for a new musical vehicle that would be accessible and beneficial to the brothers of Taizé as well as their visitors, the community encountered short canons used by a monastery in the Catalan region of Spain. The brothers adapted this form to create the first Taizé chants: "Cantate Domino," "Ubi Caritas," "Jubilate Deo," and others.[213] These first songs were often canons with Biblical texts in Latin, a "universal language" for Western Christians.

---

[212] Jason Brian Santos, *A Community Called Taizé: A Story of Prayer, Worship, and Reconciliation* (Downers Grove, Illinois: IVP Books, 2008), 105.

[213] Ibid., 107-108.

The young visitors to Taizé adopted these few songs readily, often singing each one for up to twenty minutes during informal evening prayer vigils.[214] The need for a larger repertoire of music led the community to Jacques Berthier, an organist and composer in Paris who had worked with the brothers of Taizé previously. Berthier and the brothers worked together to create new songs. The composer sent each draft to Taizé, where the brothers would sing and critique the music from the standpoint of its usefulness within the context of daily prayer. Finally, in the mid-1980's, the community substituted the new genre of chorus for its previous liturgical music, and Taizé prayer, as so many around the world have practiced it, came into being.[215]

The music of Taizé can be called song or chant or chorus. While a careful analysis of the Taizé repertoire finds four different genres of song within the corpus (canon, ostinato, litany, and acclamation), most examples of Taizé chant, regardless of genre, share many musical qualities.[216] These pieces usually include eight to twelve measures of simple music, set to a text frequently taken directly from the Bible. The texts of these songs are available in many languages, so that singers can sing in their own languages all at the same time, creating a type of peaceful and faith-filled Babel. Worshippers repeat these choruses countless times, so that the words can become absorbed into the heart rather than produced as a conscious effort of the intellect. As each song is repeated, its performance varies: new instruments enter, certain

---

[214] Ibid. While Brother Roger and the youth seemed "delighted," the brothers sometimes found the repetition to be too much.

[215] Ibid., 110.

[216] For an analysis of these four types of Taizé chant, as well as further musicological analysis, see Judith Marie Kubicki, *Liturgical Music as Ritual Symbol: A Case Study of Jacques Berthier's Taizé Music* (Leuven: Peeters, 1999), 41-91.

voices drop out, the texture thickens or thins, or a cantor adds an obbligato line. Repetition and variation equally contribute to the power of the music of Taizé.

THE ORATORY FUNCTION OF TAIZÉ AND CHARISMATIC TEXTS

The simple "songs of awe and glory" of the charismatic movement and the contemplative chants of Taizé have much in common. Both are straightforward, making use of short, direct phrases. Music leaders repeat both types of music over and over again, not counting or predetermining how many times each is performed. In music both from Taizé and the charismatic movement, musicians sing and play with one ear to the Spirit, attempting to discern when to repeat or how to vary the music for the benefit of the congregation. Leaders also fully expect God to move through Taizé chants as well as through charismatic choruses. As Jack Hayford, composer and author, writes, "Worshipping God brings the highest sense of dignity humanly can know, for the regal nature of His Majesty begins to flow downward and inward."[217]

This expectation of a divine encounter provides the key to the function of both types of music. These pieces serve as *cantio divina*: a sung spiritual discipline similar to *lectio divina*, or holy reading. The practice of holy reading, dating to the earliest centuries of Christianity, thrived especially in Benedictine religious communities. In *lectio divina*, the Christian chooses a passage of scripture and reads that passage over and over again. This reading falls into four stages. The first, *lectio* or

---

[217] Jack W. Hayford, "Worship His Majesty," in *Pentecostal and Charismatic Studies: A Reader*, ed. William K. Kay and Anne E. Dyer (London: SCM Press, 2004), 164.

reading, invites the Christian to read a passage slowly and aloud, ready to stop when a word or phrase catches the eye or the imagination. Once that word or phrase is identified, the Christian begins *meditatio*, or meditation. Here, the reader can "ruminate on it, letting the text penetrate [his or her] being through repetition and reflection."[218] This rumination provides room for God to speak connecting the phrase from scripture with the world of the reader. Then, the reader enters *oratio*, or prayer, using the scripture reading as a springboard to share heart and desires with God. The exercise ends with *contemplatio*, or contemplation. At this point, the Christian stills all words and images in an attempt simply to be present with God.

In many ways, singing a Taizé chant or a simple charismatic chorus is a similar experience to praying through *lectio divina*. A short text is repeated over and over so that the words are taken into the experience of the singer. Throughout the process, the congregation listens for God in lyrics and music and in the participation of the whole community. Participants approach this singing not as an opportunity to learn of the faith, or as a time for praising God, but as Christians practicing a spiritual discipline. The fruits of such a discipline vary; while charismatics might expect their worship to be visited visibly by the Holy Spirit, resulting in speaking in tongues and healings evident to the entire assembly, members of the Taizé community would more likely expect increased spiritual growth and the sensation of closeness to God. In the first case the practice of this musical/spiritual discipline might lead to ecstatic outbursts, while in the second it may result in contemplative silence. Although the manifestations of God's gifts differ, each form of music presupposes and encourages connection with God.

---

218 Jane Tomaine, *St. Benedict's Toolbox: The Nuts and Bolts of Everyday Benedictine Living* (Harrisburg, Pennsylvania: Morehouse, 2005), 34.

This "inner unity with God," as described on the Taizé web site, is an ongoing gift that can continue to reverberate long after the official time of prayer and singing has ended.

As in *lectio divina*, the texts for many Taizé songs come from the Bible. Singers may repeat the words of Jesus, "Stay with me, remain with me, watch and pray, watch and pray," or they may exult with Jesus' mother before his birth, "Sing out my soul, my heart rejoices in the Lord!" The congregation may echo the words of the thief on the cross, "Jesus, remember me when you come into your kingdom," or the psalmist, "Sing praises, all you people, sing praises to the Lord."

Other Taizé chants offer very simple prayers, such as "Give peace to every heart, give peace to every heart. Give peace, Lord, give peace, Lord," or "Holy Spirit, come to us." Alternately, the songs can be assuring statements of faith rather than prayers to God, as in the chant:

Nothing can trouble, nothing can frighten,
those who seek God shall never go wanting.
Nothing can trouble, nothing can frighten,
God alone fills us. [219]

Despite the rather somber reputation of Taizé prayer, its music also makes room for joyful expressions of praise and gratitude. We find these in chants such as "In the Lord rejoicing! Christ is risen from the dead! Alleluia!" and "Sing praises to the Lord. Alleluia, alleluia! Sing in joy and gladness." [220]

---

[219] Jacques Berthier, ©1986, 1991, Les Presses de Taizé, GIA Publications Inc. agent. Used by permission.

[220] All lyrics to Taizé chants mentioned on this page composed by the Taizé Community.

These direct cries of the heart are similar to the short charismatic songs of John Wimber and others. These songs may linger in simple adoration of Jesus Christ, as Wimber's song "Isn't He" does:

Isn't he beautiful?
Beautiful, isn't he?
Prince of Peace, Son of God, isn't he?

Isn't he wonderful?
Wonderful, isn't he?
Counselor, Almighty God, isn't he, isn't he, isn't he?[221]

Others reflect on the relationship between Creator and Created, a relationship strengthened through worship in song:

Abba Father, Abba Father, my soul delights in You.
Abba Father, Abba Father, my soul delights in You.
Hallelujah, my heart has cause to sing,
I'm a spirit-born, blood-bought, child of The King,
Abba Father, Abba Father, my soul delights in You.[222]

Still other songs serve as encouragements to those around to engage in intimate worship of the Creator. "Spirit Song," another composition by Wimber, acts as an encouragement to the congregation during the verses, but lapses into prayer to Jesus during the chorus:

Verse 1: O let the Son of God enfold you with his Spirit
and his love.
Let him fill your heart and satisfy your soul.
O let him have the things that hold you,
and his Spirit, like a dove,
Will descend upon your life and make you whole.

---

[221] John Wimber, © 1980 Mercy/Vineyard Publishing as found in *The Praise and Worship Fake Book* (Franklin, TN: Brentwood-Benson Music Publishing, 2003), 229. Used with permission.

[222] "Abba Father" by Chris Bowater, © copyright 1980 Sovereign Lifestyle Music Ltd. Reproduced by permission - sovereignmusic@aol.com

Chorus: Jesus, O Jesus, come and fill your lambs.
Jesus, O Jesus, come and fill your lambs.

Verse 2: O come and sing this song with gladness
   as your hearts are filled with joy.
Lift your hands in sweet surrender to his name.
O give him all your tears and sadness,
   give him all your years of pain,
and you'll enter into life in Jesus' name.[223]

Even simpler, some choruses consist of just one or two words. Video footage records Wimber himself leading the singing of a chorus made up of the single word "Jesus" following a time of musical glossolalia.[224]

George Black, in an article concerning the canons of the Taizé repertoire, compares them to another form of spiritual discipline. According to Black, the canons

> fulfill much the same function as a mantra or the Jesus Prayer... They still the agitation of the mind and prepare the singer for prayer. They may even become prayer itself. The point is not to make progress, as in discursive thought or in most kinds of music, but to focus the attention on a simple thing – in this case the loving presence of God.[225]

---

[223] "Spirit Song," by John Wimber, ©1979 Mercy Publishing. Found in *The United Methodist Hymnal* (Nashville: The United Methodist Publishing House, 1989), 347. Used with permission.

[224] www.youtube.com/watch?v=EKs5AjdtjBY accessed June 28, 2010.

[225] George Black, "Church Musician in France: Part II Canons at Taizé," *The American Organist* (July 1980): 36; quoted in Robert Rankin Brooks, "Music and Worship of the Taizé Community" (MM diss., Southwestern Baptist Theological Seminary, 1984), 53.

The Calming Role of Taizé and Charismatic Music

The music of these prayers, both charismatic and Taizé, fosters an ethos of spiritual exploration. The evolving, multi-layered accompaniments for Taizé chants, described above, create an ever-shifting, ambient atmosphere of attentiveness.[226] Such constant repetition, and the subtle musical changes that weave through it, draw attention to the quiet voice of the Spirit, a voice that could be lost amid louder and busier music. While charismatic "songs of awe and glory" do not always involve the shifting textures of Taizé chant, their quiet repetition and improvised vocal harmonies also foster an internal alertness to the presence of the Spirit.

Yet music that is created to be repeated endlessly must be worthy of repetition. These songs must be simple and accessible without becoming boring. The tunes of Wimber and other charismatic composers allow room for melodic climax and descent, for the building and release of musical energy. Their supporting chord progressions do not startle the singer in a way that would draw attention away from the meaning of the lyrics. Yet they contain just enough variety to keep from being dull or trite.

We find this in "Isn't He," a Wimber composition mentioned earlier. The melody remains in a lower range throughout the first 5 measures of the piece, then rises dramatically for the phrase "Son of God." This difference in range provides a point of interest in the piece and a climax for the singers without becoming distracting from the

---

[226] Judith Kubicki refers to the music of Taizé as *aleatory,* or to a certain extent undetermined. She finds that the aleatory quality of this music aids "the Taizé music [in situating] the assembly in a foundational role which expresses both leadership and mutuality." Kubucki, 70-75, 91.

spiritual point of the singing. Additionally, charismatic musical practice invites individual variation. Those who feel comfortable doing so improvise harmonies, adding unpredictable textual changes throughout the singing.

Jacques Bertier's music for Taizé solves the paradox of music that must be simple but not boring by employing modal scales: melodic and harmonic patterns that vary somewhat from the major and minor scales that contemporary Western European and North American ears expect. These modal elements provide aural interest in the short chord progressions that constitute Taizé chants. An example of this is found in Berthier's "Bless the Lord, My Soul" (see Example 1).

Example 1[227]

[227] Jacques Berthier, © 1991, Les Presses de Taizé, GIA Publications Inc. agent. Found in *Songs and Prayers of Taizé* (Chicago: GIA Publications, 1991), 7. Used with permission.

The piece is in D minor, a key signature that requires B flats. Yet the second chord of the composition is a G major chord, employing a B natural rather than a B flat. This is subtly unexpected; the G major chord opens up the congregation's expectations, a sensation which is reinforced when the same chord progression occurs four measures later. Such an unusual harmonic turn provides just enough interest to maintain musical appeal over frequent repetition, yet not enough to distract singers from their prayer. And just as singers might ponder different implications of the prayer at each repetition, they also may explore different musical aspects of the song. They may shift from singing melody to alto or tenor or bass. They may sing first in English, then in Latin. They might cease singing entirely in order to listen, or to hum. Each of these methods opens up a new path of participation, just as each repetition of the prayer may open up a new spiritual insight.

SCRIPTURAL INSTANCES OF MUSIC AS *CANTIO DIVINA*

Practitioners of charismatic and Taizé music seek to use their singing in order to draw close to God. Of vital importance in both styles of music is the activity of the Holy Spirit in worship. Charismatics are justifiably famous for their emphasis on the movement of the Spirit. Yet those who engage in Taizé prayer also rely on the Spirit to guide and enliven their worship. Chants such as "Spirit of Christ Jesus," "Holy Spirit, loving Spirit," "Holy Spirit, Come to Us," and "Come and pray in us, Holy Spirit," testify to the pneumatology of worship that the Taizé community maintains. We can understand the role of the Spirit in worship better by looking at two New Testament passage for insight into the actions and nature of the third person of the Trinity, particularly as they intersect with worship.

Jesus' explains to the Samaritan woman at the well, in John 4:23, that "true worshippers will worship the Father in spirit and truth." Yet what does it mean to worship in spirit and truth? While it may be tempting to interpret this as a call to "inner" worship, especially in contrast to the concrete locations for worship mentioned in verses 20-21, scholars caution against such an internal-external dichotomy. As used in this passage in the Gospel of John, spirit "does not mean [our] soul or understanding, that which is most like God in [us], [our] immaterial or purely inward part... it denotes the reality of God... this reality is to be found only in Jesus."[228] Moreover, the Spirit makes possible the eschatological facets of worship implied in Jesus' statement that "the hour is coming, and is now here:" in true spirited worship, we experience the reality of God's presence with us, a foretaste of the eternal joy of God's presence at the end of time. This brief passage highlights the relational, eschatological, and vital character of the Spirit's influence in worship. It also sheds light on the *cantio divina* of Taizé chants and charismatic choruses. Here, we see the Spirit not as the source of chaos but as the living reality of God. Music that serves to help worshippers draw near to and become aware of that reality is truly Spirit-led.

Earlier in the Gospel of John, Jesus shares another conversation about the Spirit, this time with Nicodemus. Jesus counsels Nicodemus that in order to see the kingdom of God, he must be born[229] from above, of the Spirit. Here, the Spirit's active role is affirmed; just as parents conceive and bear the child, the Spirit creates us anew as children of God.

---

[228] Gerhard Kittel and Gerhard Friedrich, ed., *Theological Dictionary of the New Testament*, trans. Geoffrey W. Bromiley (Grand Rapids: Eerdmans, 1968) 6:439.

[229] The Greek here could imply either being born (as from a mother) or being begotten (as from a father).

This passage reminds us that it is God who draws close to us in worship. No charismatic chorus or Taizé chant can produce that proximity. Rather, the singing of contemplative or ecstatic music may help us become aware of the Spirit who is already close to us.

Another aspect of music in these traditions is their relationship to silence. As the Taizé community explains:

> Remaining silent, we trust and hope in God. One psalm suggests that silence is even a form of praise. We are used to reading at the beginning of Psalm 65: "Praise is due to you, O God". This translation follows the Greek text, but actually the Hebrew text printed in most Bibles reads: "Silence is praise to you, O God". When words and thoughts come to an end, God is praised in silent wonder and admiration.[230]

Charismatics, likewise, can descend into depths of stillness as worshippers "wait upon the Lord" and allow the Spirit to intercede with "sighs too deep for words." This last passage, from chapter 8 of the letter to the Romans, provides another scriptural insight into charismatic and Taizé music. Both Taizé and charismatic practices allow the worshipper freedom to sing or not sing, to hum or fall silent, to participate in prayer and music as each individual is led. Both traditions have great respect for the intercessions of the Spirit that happen when we cease making sound. As Elijah did in 1 Kings 19, worshippers may find God's presence in quietude rather than in explosive and exciting noise. The gentle repetitions in each tradition may lead worshippers ultimately to a place of peace and silent communion with God.

In his second letter to the Corinthians, Paul explained, "Now the Lord is the Spirit, and where the Spirit of the Lord is, there is freedom. And all of us, with unveiled faces, seeing the glory of the Lord as though reflected in a mirror, are being transformed into the same image from

---

[230] www.taize.fr/en_article12.html accessed June 28, 2010.

146

one degree of glory to another; for this comes from the Lord, the Spirit" (vs17-18). Paul highlights, in these verses, the freedom that the Spirit gives to encounter God in a more direct and life-changing manner. He believes that such freedom should result in "boldness" in seeking after God and participating in the transformation into the image of Christ. This freedom in the pursuit of God is evident in charismatic and Taizé music, where musicians must constantly make unscripted choices, taking into account the singing of the congregation and the leading of the Spirit. Neither Taizé chant nor charismatic performance practice designate the number of repetitions, dynamic levels, the entrance of obbligato voices or instruments, the number of musical leaders, or even which instruments might be used. Faced with an infinite number of musical options, leaders rely on the Spirit to guide them in responding to congregational singing as they decide to make another repeat, add or subtract an instrument, or change the musical texture in some other way. In both styles of worship, the goal of the *cantio divina*, or holy singing, is drawing close to God in order to be transformed "from one degree of glory to another." The unfixed and improvisational aspects of Taizé and charismatic music allow for musical responsiveness to the spiritual discipline of the congregation's singing. And that discipline has as its goal "to know Jesus better, to follow him more closely, to become – in some mysterious way – wrapped into his presence."[231]

Finally, one cannot help but note the importance of repetition within each of these musical traditions. The practice and effects of such repetition have been described above. Yet it is curious to note how they are consistent with scriptural tradition as seen in the Psalms and elsewhere. The Psalter frequently makes use of repetition, the most

---

[231] Tony Jones, *The Sacred Way: Spiritual Practices for Everyday Life* (Grand Rapids: Zondervan, 2005), 16-17.

spectacular example of which is found in Psalm 136. The phrase "for his steadfast love endures forever" responds to the first part of every verse in the psalm, for a total of twenty-six iterations. We find more subtle examples of recurrence, known as synonymous parallelism, throughout the Psalter. This literary technique involves restating a given theme or sentiment in two related versions. We find several examples of synonymous parallelism in Psalm 120. In the second verse, the psalmist pleads, "'Deliver me, O Lord, from lying lips, from a deceitful tongue,'" effectively repeating the idea of "lying lips" yet using different vocabulary to convey the same idea. Again, in verse 3, we find another repetition: "What shall be given to you? And what more shall be done to you, you deceitful tongue?" The question gains in emphasis due to its restatement. The answer, likewise, comes in a synonymous parallelism: "A warrior's sharp arrows, with glowing coals of the broom tree!" While arrows and coals are not identical, both bring pain or punishment, and therefore function similarly. We find a final instance of synonymous parallelism in verse 5, when the psalmist grieves: "Woe is me, that I am an alien in Meshech, that I must live among the tents of Kedar." The repetition here compounds the sense of alienation. Each of these restatements functions much like the repetitions do within the musical traditions of charismatics and Taizé : repetition is rarely musically exact, but serves to deepen the theme by varying it slightly while maintaining the core sentiment of each song or chant.

CRITICISM OF MUSIC AS *CANTIO DIVINA*

Although Taizé prayer and charismatic worship have much in common musically, complaints about the worship and music practices of these traditions usually center specifically on one of the two genres. We will first explore critiques of charismatic music and worship, and then turn to those of Taizé.

In his response to an apology for charismatic worship, Paul Zahl shares a sharply-worded criticism of this tradition. The problem, he writes,

> was its emphasis on victory rather than on redemption, on victorious living rather than on *simul iustus et peccator*... The charismatic movement blew it because it wanted to pole-vault over Calvary on the way to Pentecost. (Who does not?) It flew right over the unevangelized dark continents of the Christian heart. It underestimated the awesome devastating force of inherited and continuing sin.[232]

Certainly, many of the charismatic musical examples cited above seem victorious rather than penitential. Likewise, it is true that song as spiritual discipline seeks to draw the worshipper into closer communion with God, and therefore into a more righteous way of life. Yet the spiritual disciplines evolved as practices to help a fallen humanity wrestle with "inherited and continuing sin." Were the heart always pure, fasting and meditation and pilgrimage and *lectio divina* would not be required to return our attention to the One we need. Seen in this light, charismatic music is a practice that serves as a bulwark against the temptations of sin. Although the lyrics of many charismatic songs are optimistic and assured, the practice of singing them wages war against the power of evil.

One may argue that the root of such disciplines is not visible to most charismatics; no matter the reason that spiritual practices originated, people will not face the death, and Christ's death, that comes as a wage of sin unless brought to that topic explicitly by the words they sing or speak or hear. It is true that Calvary is as much a part of the Christian story as Easter and Pentecost are. Sin, confession, and forgiveness are as much a component of human living as sanctification

---

[232] Paul Zahl, "A Liturgical Worship Response" in *Exploring the Worship Spectrum*, ed. Paul Basden (Grand Rapids: Zondervan: 2004), 154.

and transformation into the image of Christ. Yet these darker topics do not feature as prominently in the choruses and sung worship of charismatic traditions. Whether this means that such topics are absent from charismatic worship, however, is another question. As mentioned at the beginning of this book, many traditions may include functions or themes within another component of worship than music. Thus charismatic preachers might include explorations of human sin and Christ's sacrifice, while times of prayer may include opportunities for confession, even though these may not appear within the charismatic musical canon.

Another fear of those outside the charismatic tradition is that so much focus on the third person of the Trinity will result in less attention paid to the second person. Both Harold Best and Sally Morganthaler voice concern that Christ's critical importance and work not be overshadowed in charismatic worship by concern for the Spirit's activity. Just as Christ's actions on the cross and in the tomb are critical for a full expression of Christianity, as described above, the person of Christ must feature prominently in Christian worship. Morgenthaler cites a recent study of popular songs from charismatic worship, finding only thirteen out of two hundred that "focused on the work or person of Christ."[233] She notes that this is of particular concern, given the great proportion of time spent singing in charismatic worship.

Finally, critics have traditionally worried about the freedom inherent in charismatic worship, a freedom that has the potential to become disorderly. The apostle Paul gives an early version of this worry when he cautions the Christians in Corinth that "all things should be

---

[233] Sally Morgenthaler, "An Emerging Worship Response," in *Exploring the Worship Spectrum*, ed. Paul Basden (Grand Rapids: Zondervan, 2004), 169. Also, Harold Best, "A Traditional Worship Response. " in *Exploring*, 158.

done decently and in order." When discussing the charismatic worship tradition with a class recently, I found many of my students shared the concern that the freedom of such Spirit-led worship could lead to chaos, and that this would result in confusion for those from outside the tradition. Some students also discerned that charismatic worship might appeal to more extroverted Christians, while doing little to invite more timid or introverted worshippers.

These concerns can be allayed in part by the recognition that human ritual, no matter how open to the workings of the Spirit, inevitably takes a fixed shape. While charismatic worship patterns may be interrupted periodically by unexpected messages or occurrences, these patterns nonetheless become familiar. As James F. White notes, "a programed order of worship is often alien, although familiar patterns develop and predictability is rather high."[234]

Taizé prayer draws an entirely different set of criticisms. Students who have attended worship services in this style often complain about the amount of repetition. A very few words are sung very many times, and this practice can frustrate some. Such repetition can leave those looking for an objective trajectory of thought about God in the lurch. When the singer does not find a way to let this repetition work as a spiritual practice, it becomes boring and meaningless. As the Taizé community itself admits, "The 'songs of Taizé' published in different languages are simple, but preparation is required to use them in prayer."[235] Aside from the musical preparation of having competent leaders and a congregation familiar with the songs or willing and able to

---

[234] James F. White, *Protestant Worship: Traditions in Transition* (Louisville: Westminster John Knox Press, 1989), 198.

[235] www.taize.fr/en_article338.html accessed June 29, 2010.

read them in a songbook or bulletin, spiritual preparation makes the music of Taizé "work." This preparation might include quieting thoughts and body, slowing down one's internal rhythms, beginning to attend to small and subtle details, and relaxing into an attitude open to simplicity and repetition. As such, this worship style may become a stumbling block to those unprepared for its quiet rigor.

Another common complaint from first-time attendees at Taizé prayer is the soporific effect of its combination of silence, quiet readings, and droning, circling music. Such an atmosphere of peace can easily lead to unintentional naps in this over-worked and sleep-deprived American culture. Some may argue that worshipers need something to attract their attention rather than to lull them into hazy inattention, particularly at a time when so many things compete so loudly and brightly for our attention. Others would counter that the Church ought to provide a haven from overstimulation and training in the ability to focus and abide in quietude, even if (or especially if) all other institutions have forsaken these ways of being. As daily life becomes more and more filled with media and technology that alert us to each new e-mail, text message, public scandal, or entertainment event, the question of whether worship should participate in or protest this bombardment grows in importance. While the community of Taizé does factor culture, language, and the practices of worshippers into its decisions concerning worship (as evidenced by the community's adoption of short canons rather than the varieties of French liturgical music it previously employed in order to allow non-Francophones to more easily participate in worship), the brothers have adopted a strong stance regarding the need of the church at worship to be set apart from the activity of the day. Such a posture may prove prophetic for the Christian Church of the twenty-first century.

INTRODUCING THIS FUNCTION INTO THE WORSHIP OF OTHER TRADITIONS

Although many congregations may be attracted by the heart-felt simplicity of charismatic choruses or the meditative peace of Taizé chants, these forms of music can be troublesome to introduce because of the difficulties they present for musicians. Many church musicians, as is true of many musicians outside the church, practice diligently in order to maintain control of a performance. Musicians tend to find comfort in knowing how many stanzas of a hymn will be sung, or how many times a chorus of a praise song will be repeated. Yet Taizé and charismatic music operate on the premise that the musician does not know how often a song will be repeated, or exactly what musical changes may occur throughout the piece. Musicians in this style strive to be attentive to the moving of the Spirit and the practice of the congregation, and they attempt to modify their accompanying in response to these things. Those unused to this way of making music can respond in fear and disbelief when told, "We don't know how many times we'll sing and play this piece." Overcoming the urge to standardize and predetermine each performance is an important step in bringing charismatic and Taizé music into the worshipping practices of a congregation.

Congregation members often have little difficulty following the free and improvisatory evolution of charismatic songs and Taizé chants. Since they are accustomed to following the music leaders in any case, they generally find little difference when trusting their leaders through the Spirit-led repetitions of this repertoire. The difficulty for the congregation may come in allowing music to serve a different role in worship. If congregations expect their singing to be didactic, responsorial, testimonial, or doxological, they may find that Taizé chants and charismatic choruses take unfamiliar directions. Pastors and worship leaders may need to encourage congregations to consider music as a form of prayer, rather than as an action of worship separate from prayer. Indeed, Christians have sung their prayers since the earliest days of the Church. The Psalter contains many of the earliest song-prayers of Christian believers. But the Western Church has lost the unity of song and prayer.

The easiest way to encourage congregations in this understanding of their music might be to replace a traditional prayer time with a sung form of prayer that accomplishes the same thing. For example, a congregation that regularly lifts up petitions for the world around it might use the Taizé prayer refrain "Kyrie, Kyrie, eleison" during this time.[236]

This refrain precedes each petition; at the end of the refrain, the congregation continues to hold the final notes on a neutral vowel or by humming the pitches. As the congregation holds these notes, a cantor or prayer leader may offer up a petition, either spoken or sung. At the end of the petition, the congregation shifts to the next chord, and prepares to sing the refrain again.

---

[236] Jacques Berthier, "Kyrie Eleison 10," copyright 1991, Les Presses de Taizé, GIA Publications Inc. agent. Found in in *Songs & Prayers from Taizé* (Chicago: GIA Publications, 1991), 2. Used with permission. A recording of this refrain alternating with sung petitions is found at www.youtube.com/watch?v=mgY0jQykj8E

Another example of this technique might involve the prayer of confession and words of assurance. Following a spoken or silent confession of sins, the congregation might slowly and quietly begin singing "I Am a Friend of God," a repetitive song in the charismatic vein with only one verse, inspired by verses 4 and 5 of Psalm 8.

Verse: Who am I that you are mindful of me,
That you hear me when I call?
Is it true that you are thinking of me?
How you love me, it's amazing.
Chorus: I am a friend of God, I am a friend of God.
I am a friend of God, He calls me friend.[237]

Used in this way, the song continues the people's prayer, yet moves the intention from confession to receiving assurance of God's forgiveness and steadfast love. The lyrics articulate the Christian's grateful astonishment that sin can be forgiven and that God treats us as friends rather than servants, however much such friendship might feel undeserved.

Such inclusions of singing at expected times of prayer can help the congregation understand the words it sings, and the action of singing itself, as a form of prayer. Once this point has been reached, worship leaders can expand the opportunities and reasons for prayer, from petitions and prayers of forgiveness to prayer as a practice to help us become more aware of the presence of God.

Each of the traditions studied thus far have originated in Western European practices of Christianity and music-making. Yet the worship practices of many North American congregations have also

---

[237] Michael Gungor and Israel Houghton, © 2003 Integrity Worship Music (Admin. by Capitol CMG Publishing. Used with permission. Found at www.lyricsmode.com/lyrics/i/israel_houghton/i_am_a_friend_of_god. html accessed June 6, 2012.

been affected by the worship and music of Western Africa, as present in African American spirituals and gospel songs. We will now turn to these genres of music, and their function as vehicles for truth-telling in the context of worship.

CHAPTER 7: SINGING IN THE AFRICAN-AMERICAN SPIRITUALS TRADITION
SONG AS TRUTH-TELLING

The way in which we worshipped is almost indescribable. The singing
was accompanied by a certain ecstasy of motion, clapping of hands,
tossing of heads, which would continue without cessation about half an
hour; one would lead off in a kind of recitative style, others joining in the
chorus. The old house partook of the ecstasy; it rang with their jubilant
shouts, and shook in all its joints.[238]

Hope, in the black spirituals, is not a denial of history. Black hope
accepts history, but believes that the historical is in motion, moving
toward a divine fulfillment. It is the belief that things can be radically
otherwise than they are: that reality is not fixed, but is moving in the
direction of human liberation.[239]

The African-American Church has gifted Christianity with an
amazing assortment of music for worship: spirituals, meter music,
gospel songs, R&B, and even hip-hop and other emerging forms. What is
true of all of the other traditions mentioned in this work is doubly true
of African-American music: great variety exists among composers, styles,
intents, and functions of music. Although many nineteenth-century
gospel songs share testimony of God's action in the life of an individual,
not all do. Likewise, although praise is a central topic for very many
songs from the CWM field, it is not the only theme. This caution needs to

---

[238] David Smith, *The Biography of Rev. David Smith* (Xenia, Ohio: 1881), 162-163.

[239] James H. Cone, *The Spirituals and the Blues: An Interpretation* (New York:
Seabury Press, 1972), 95-96.

be repeated at the beginning of this chapter. The enormous variety of styles of African-American worship music, and the huge number of different songs within each style, makes finding a single purpose of such music-making practically impossible. Spirituals can retell Bible stories, interpret contemporary life in spiritual terms, enter into exuberant praise, encourage in times of great difficulty, and work in many other ways. But in this chapter we will focus on a function of music that is rarely found in the other genres of music discussed previously. We will examine African-American music, and particularly the spirituals of this community, as an exercise in truth-telling in the face of difficulty, a truth-telling that results in lamentation and protest.

THE HISTORY OF MUSIC IN AFRICAN-AMERICAN CHRISTIAN WORSHIP

The roots of African-American worship music rest, of course, in West African soil. Slaves, torn from their home and violently carried to the American colonies, retained the musical traditions of their homeland. These traditions include an understanding of music as something that expresses, simultaneously, both sacred and secular realities, in contrast to the way that sacred and secular have traditionally been divided in Western European cultures.[240] In addition, music in West Africa implied a rich stew of vocal and instrumental and dance art forms. These aspects of performance all contributed to music, rather than functioning as separate and isolated disciplines. One sees the persistence of this integral combination in the description of singing spirituals during worship at the beginning of this chapter: movement and percussive

---

[240] Indeed, not just music but all of African life incorporated the sacred and the secular. See Melva Wilson Costen, *African-American Christian Worship* (Nashville: Abingdon Press, 1993), 17.

hand-clapping as well as vocal production all contribute to the music-making. Instruments in West Africa could be found in many forms: aerophones, chordophones, idiophones, and membranophones were all common, despite the frequent assumption that drums were the only instruments available to Africans.[241] West African music employed melody and harmonies, but it was and is particularly marked by polyrhythm: the simultaneous presence of two or more different rhythmic patterns. These factors strongly affected the music that the slaves would make upon arrival in the Americas.[242]

Most of the roughly one million African slaves brought to the American colonies ended up in the South. Life for them included the tragedies of slavery: families members separated and sold, enforced illiteracy, physical and emotional abuse, prohibitions against traditional African religions, a denial of Christian baptism for those who chose to follow the new religion, and slave masters' refusal to allow cultural artifacts from West Africa, such as musical instruments. Despite such horrific treatment, slaves developed a rich musical culture. One noticeable component of this culture included work songs. These vocal creations, also called hollers and calls, coordinated the rhythm of tasks at home and in the field. The texts of these work songs could describe

---

[241] According to the Hornbostel-Sachs taxonomy, used by most ethnomusicologists, instruments can be divided into four categories: those that produce sound through blown air (such as a clarinet), those that produce sound by the vibration of strings (such as a piano), those that produce sound by themselves vibrating (such as a tambourine or maracas), and those that produce sound through the vibration of a membrane (such as a timpani).

[242] Terry E. Miller and Andrew Shahriari, *World Music: A Global Journey*, 2nd ed. (New York: Routledge, 2006), 274. Chapter 10 provides a useful overview of African musical traditions from several parts of the continent.

the job being performed or might include religions imagery and theological statements.

Other musical forms were kept hidden from unsympathetic white slave owners. The ring shout developed as a secretive religious and musical ritual. Slaves gathered secretly at night in secluded places, often called "brush arbors" or "hush arbors." There, participants formed a ring and shuffled or stepped or danced counterclockwise around the circle, keeping time to improvised vocal music.[243] According to popular superstition, a washtub might be placed in the center of the ring to catch the sound of the worship and prevent discovery by outsiders.[244] The music of these ring shouts gave birth to what is now known as the African-American spiritual.

Spirituals are marked by several features. 1) They are deeply biblical, combining texts and metaphors from the New Testament and especially the Old Testament to make sense of contemporary life. 2) Their message is one of long-lasting import, in two senses. Many spirituals speak of heaven and eternal life, giving them a timeless quality. But no matter their subject, spirituals seem to speak as directly and truthfully to modern-day Christians as they did to the slaves that first created them. 3) The melodies of spirituals are marked by rhythmic interest, including syncopations, dotted rhythms, and dramatic pauses. 4) Melodically, they tend to follow pentatonic patterns (using the first, second, third, fifth, and sixth notes of a major scale, but avoiding the fourth and seventh notes; one can simulate a pentatonic scale by playing the black notes on a piano keyboard). 5) They also betray improvisatory

---

[243] Melva Costen offers a fuller description of ring shouts as they featured in later praise houses in *African American Christian Worship*, 52-54.

[244] Ibid., 38.

beginnings, especially in their repetitive nature. When creating a new song on the spot, it is very helpful to repeat a line once or twice while searching for a new phrase to sing. The repetition evident in so many spirituals remains as an artifact of this immediate creation while in the heat of worship. 6) Spirituals are also frequently antiphonal; they incorporate a call-and-response technique that hints at different roles for the leader and the group. 7) Listeners can often identify coded meanings in the texts of spirituals; "crossing the Jordan" might instruct runaway slaves to cross rivers in order to obscure their scent from the dogs of slave owners, for example. 8) Finally, spirituals were meant to be sung heterophonically. The same melody could be sung in slightly different ways by many different singers at the same time. This results in a "messy", loose performance that might be uncomfortable for listeners accustomed to rigid uniformity. Each of these characteristics contributed to the unique power and beauty of the spirituals, and also to the continuing growth of African-American worship music forms.[245]

Not all African-Americans resided in the South, however. A growing number of freed slaves, and of African-Americans who had never been slaves, formed communities in the Northern colonies, which became the Northern states. These escaped the hopeless slavery of the South, but their lives were nonetheless subject to exclusion, discrimination, and danger. At first included in white religious movements and denominations in the North, African-Americans were slowly moved both literally and metaphorically from the sanctuary to the balcony to outside the church building. They naturally grew impatient with such unchristian behavior and began to form their own

---

[245] I am indebted in this description of the musical and lyrical aspects of spirituals to Wyatt Tee Walker, *Somebody's Calling My Name: Black Sacred Music and Social Change* (Valley Forge: Judson Press, 1992), 52-59.

congregations and denominations where African-American participation and leadership were welcomed.[246]

While we might be tempted to associate spirituals with all African-American congregations and communities, these songs of faith from out of slavery were often shunned by African-Americans in the North.[247] Northern congregations tended instead to sing hymns popular with white congregations, including the texts of Isaac Watts and Charles Wesley. These, however, were sung quite differently. Contemporary accounts of singing in Northern African-American congregations mention moaning, antiphonal performance of hymns, and improvisation woven into the singing. In many instances, the technique of "lining out" hymns flourished: the song leader intoned the first line of a hymn, and then led the congregation in singing the words. While lining-out had been popular in white congregations in the Colonies in the eighteenth century, the practice retained its usefulness and popularity in African-American churches into the twentieth century, in some places. Such African-American use of Western European hymns gained the names "meter music" or "metered music" or "improvised hymns."[248]

---

[246] For more detailed information concerning the foundation dates and particularities of African-American congregations and denominations, see Costen, *African American Christian Worship*, 83-117.

[247] Daniel Alexander Payne, a Bishop in the African Methodist Episcopal Church, for example, openly showed his disdain for such practices in his autobiography. He recalls attending a "bush meeting" around 1878, during which he witnessed worshippers who "clapped their hands and stamped their feet in a most ridiculous and heathenish way. [He] requested the pastor to go and stop their dancing... to desist and to sit down and to sing in a rational manner." Payne also calls the ring shout "disgusting" and "ignorant." Albert J. Raboteau, *Slave Religion: The "Invisible Institution" in the Antebellum South* (New York: Oxford University Press, 1978), 68-69.

[248] Costen, 98-100.

Following the Civil War, however, the popularity of spirituals began to spread throughout the United States and even abroad. The Fisk Jubilee Singers, from African-American Fisk University, performed fund-raising concerts in Northern cities during the second half of the nineteenth century. The ensemble slowly added spirituals to their program in addition to the traditional European concert music they performed. Wealthy audiences were deeply moved by the beautiful performances of the Fisk students as well as by the unexpected charm of non-European music.

While the Jubilee Singers and similar ensembles introduced upper-class Americans to the repertoire of spirituals, poorer audiences grew to know and appreciate spirituals through their performance by "black face" vaudeville performers. Despite the derogatory intentions of most minstrel shows toward African-American culture, some former slaves began to offer their own "black face" shows, out-performing their white counterparts and earning respect for the skills and the culture of African-Americans.[249]

The Great Migration brought about another form of African-American music. As millions of former slaves moved North in search of

---

[249] For a deeper exploration of the issues of racism, the "trickster" tradition of subverting stereotypes, and white audience expectations, see Patricia Bradley, *Making American Culture: a Social History, 1900-1920* (Basingstoke, Hampshire: Palgrave Macmillan, 2009), 18-23. Although the first iterations of black-face in minstrelsy and vaudeville are long past, black-face continues to appear in cartoons created in the mid-twentieth century (and still airing periodically on television), as well as in current events: in May of 2012 a Colorado second-grader caused a stir when arriving at school in black-face in order to make a presentation about Martin Luther King, Jr. While some found this instance of face-painting unsettling or insulting, others believed that it showed the young boy's admiration for the Civil Rights hero. These differing opinions reflect the multitude of ways in which earlier audiences and performers understood black-face within the context of minstrelsy and vaudeville.

greater opportunity, they found themselves excluded from both white communities and Northern African-American communities, which tended to look down upon their rural and illiterate Southern peers. African-Americans new to the North found solace in Pentecostal and Holiness congregations, where worship music employed a rich combination of African-American secular musical styles such as ragtime, jazz, and blues, as well as the instruments usually associated with such music: pianos, guitars, and percussion. African-American gospel music arose from these roots, marrying the exciting music of secular Black culture with the religious content of the spirituals. As described in Chapter four, the Reverend Charles Albert Tindley brought his education, artistry, and insight to crafting gospel songs that reflected the concerns of African-American life and faith at the turn of the century. In the 1930s, blues pianist-turned-Christian musician Thomas Andrew Dorsey composed and recorded "optimistic, uplifting songs" with a blues- and jazz-influenced musical language in the face of the Great Depression.[250] Singer Mahalia Jackson became the voice and face of gospel music, releasing her powerful voice and emphatic, improvisatory style first to black audiences in the 1940s, then to white audiences in the 1950s and 1960s. Each of these artists created differing iterations of gospel music and shared this music with congregations and audiences around the world.

African-American worship for music continues to grow and change. Modern gospel performers seek to combine the sounds of today's secular music (R&B, rap, hip hop) with the good news of Jesus Christ. Kirk Franklin, Israel Houghton, and Mary Mary, as well as dozens of other artists, contribute to this evolution.

---

[250] Don Cusic, "The Development of Gospel Music," in *The Cambridge Companion to Blues and Gospel Music*, ed. Allan Moore (New York: Cambridge University Press, 2002), 53.

THE FUNCTION OF LAMENT AND PROTEST IN SPIRITUALS

Spirituals provide opportunities for truth-telling that the outside culture may not welcome. The history of the African-American people of the United States is such that they were unable to tell the truth of their misery to most members of the majority culture around them. The Church was the one place that centered African-American culture: a place where truth could be shared with an understanding community and a compassionate God.

Sometimes this truth took the form of lament. In these cases, simply being able to share the difficulty and misery of daily life gave congregations the strength to go on. "Standing in the Need of Prayer" insists straight-forwardly on the singer's hardship, a state which only God, through prayer, can amend. The congregation gives voice to a powerful metaphor for loneliness in "Sometimes I Feel Like a Motherless Child," reminding itself at the end that when life is so bleak, one must "get down on my knees and pray." "Nobody Knows the Trouble I've Seen"[251] expresses the difficulty in sharing experiences of pain and sorrow with those who have not experienced such struggles. After repeating its opening line several times, the spiritual seems to enter into a *non sequitur*; "Glory, hallelujah!" follows hard upon the confession of difficulty of sharing troubles. Here, the pain of everyday life is juxtaposed with a faith in Jesus strong enough to elicit praise even in the dreariest moments. "There is a Balm" uses two techniques to bring comfort to the singer. First, modern troubles are put in the scriptural context of Jeremiah, the prophet who seeks healing for the people of God. Then, the encouraging role of the Holy Spirit is mentioned in hopes of imminent comfort.

---

[251] Sometimes this spiritual appears as "Nobody Knows the Trouble I See."

165

Other spirituals use the opportunity of truth-telling to speak words of protest to the culture around them. Often, the Church provided the only place where such protests could be safely voiced. Most of the early protest songs wrestle with the institution of slavery. In the face of this horror, African-Americans sang out "Let my people go!" with righteous indignation. By employing the metaphor of Moses demanding that Pharaoh free the Hebrew slaves, African-American slaves could protest the sin of slavery in their time and place. "Oh, Freedom" let each singer take a firm stance: "And before I'd be a slave, I'll be buried in my grave, and go home to my Lord, and be free." The assurance of ultimate freedom at the end of time allowed African-Americans to fight against their lack of freedom in the antebellum South. African-Americans continued to employ such religious protest songs in the twentieth century outside the Church when agitating for civil rights. One of these later songs, adapted from an earlier spiritual, made African-American protesters the spiritual descendants of the Hebrews entering Canaan after fleeing from Egypt. In its updated version, this song helps singers declaim "Ain't gonna let nobody/segregation/ police dogs/ tear gas turn me 'round." The most familiar of such protest songs was sung in the 1960's at sit-ins and marches: "We Shall Overcome." The words to this timeless cry share a hard-won optimism that despite human sin and the forces of evil, God's ways of justice and peace shall have the final say.[252]

---

[252] The origins to "We Shall Overcome" are somewhat murky. Possible sources which include a 1901 gospel hymn composed by Charles Albert Tindley entitled "I'll Overcome Someday," the hymn tune SICILIAN MARINERS, and Zilphia Horton and the Highlander Folk School. See Carlton R. Young, *Companion to the United Methodist Hymnal* (Nashville: Abingdon, 1993), 679-680; Troy A. Murphy, "Rhetorical Invention and the Transformation of 'We Shall Overcome,'" *Qualitative Research Reports in Communication* 4 (2003): 1.

This function of spirituals exists to a lesser extent in African-American gospel music. Some early gospel songs did reflect the difficulty of the African-American experience, juxtaposing laments with words of encouragement and trust in God. Charles Albert Tindley composed the following Gospel song as his congregation wrestled to raise money and purchase a new church building:

> We are tossed and driven on the restless sea of time,
> Somber skies and howling tempests oft succeed a bright
>   sunshine;
> In that land of perfect day, when the mists have rolled away,
> We will understand it better by and by.
>
> We are often destitute of the things that life demands,
> Want of food and want of shelter, thirsty hills and barren lands;
> We are trusting in the Lord, and according to God's word,
> We will understand it better by and by.
>
> Trials dark on every hand, and we cannot understand
> All the ways that God would lead us to that blessed promised
>   land;
> But he guides us with his eye, and we'll follow till we die,
> For we'll understand it better by and by.
>
> Temptations, hidden snares often take us unawares,
> And our hearts are made to bleed for a thoughtless word or
>   deed;
> And we wonder why the test when we try to do our best,
> But we'll understand it better by and by.[253]

While such honesty tends to serve as a counterpoint to the joyful testimonial and doxological nature of much Gospel music, it continues the thread of truth-telling begun in the Spirituals.

---

[253] "We'll Understand it Better By and By" by Charles Albert Tindley, as found in *The United Methodist Hymnal* (Nashville: The United Methodist Publishing House, 1989), 525. For background information on the hymn, see Young, 684.

Contemporary Gospel musicians are also less apt to include honest descriptions of pain and difficulty than their spiritual-singing ancestors, yet even today this thread appears. Kirk Franklin seems to have taken on the mantle of this truth-telling music in his corpus of songs. On his 2007 album *The Fight of My Life*, Franklin grieves over "Chains... of abuse, of suicide, pain from my past... chains of divorce, addiction and fear, being afraid to die and afraid to live."[254] More recently, he dedicates his song "I Smile" to "recession, depression, and unemployment," admitting that "there is no sunshine, nothing but clouds and it's dark in my heart and it feels like a cold night."[255] Scholar and preacher Brad Braxton cautions modern churches, musicians, and worship leaders not to lose the function of protest within African-American worship:

> The best elements of the African-American Christian tradition have also reminded us that these moments of spiritual ecstasy were never simply ends unto themselves. Fervent worship in our tradition has been a vehicle of deep communion with God that has brought the necessary spiritual empowerment and psychic release to enable us to ward off the powers that would hinder and dehumanize us. That is what our churches should be about, when we gather to worship.[256]

---

[254] "Chains" by Kirk Franklin, released on his recording *The Fight of My Life*, Gospo Centric, 2007. CD.

[255] "I Smile," by Kirk Franklin, released on his recording *Hello Fear*, Gospo Centric 2011. CD.

[256] Brad Ronnell Braxton, "A Good Time or a Good Life? The Black Church in the Twenty-First Century," in *Spiritual Manifestos: Visions for Renewed Religious Life in America from Young Spiritual Leaders of Many Faiths*, ed. Niles Elliot Goldstein (Woodstock, VT: Skylight Paths Publishing, 1999), 145. Ironically, Braxton contrasts his desire for the relationship between worship and protest to a 1997 Kirk Franklin song, "Stomp," which, according to Braxton, is about "making more noise than making a spiritual difference."

These functions of lamentation and protest are evident in the rich description of one African-American congregation offered by scholar Mary McGann. McGann sought to create a "liturgical ethnography," and spent years worshipping with the congregation of Our Lady of Lourdes, an African-American Catholic church in San Francisco, in order to gain experience and understanding of that congregation's practice and perception of worship and music . McGann lifts up several functions of music in her study of the worship of that community, including cultivating joy, weaving the congregation's culture into the historic forms of Roman Catholic worship, providing familiarity, and sharing the Gospel message. Yet she continually references the music's ability to raise problems with honesty and faith in the context of worship. From the very beginning of her study, she recognizes the community's "comfort with both suffering and joy. Struggle is considered a normal part of life and is meant to be shared."[257] Music often becomes the locus where suffering and joy mingle. McGann finds that "the lyrics of the community's gospel repertoire fuse the predicaments of daily living with the hope-filled images of the Scriptures."[258] Such a fusion is both of-the-minute and a reflection of the historical role of African-American religious music, which is

> crafted of cherished images at once Biblical and rooted in the historical experience of African-Americans. Beginning with the unspeakable hardships of slavery, belief that "A change is gonna come," that God 's deliverance would win out over injustice, has welled up in the voiced lyrics of the Spirituals, freedom songs

---

[257] Mary E. McGann, *A Precious Fountain: Music in the Worship of an African-American Catholic Community* (Collegeville, Minnesota: Liturgical Press, 2004), xxxi.

[258] Ibid., 20.

and gospel music, fueling the imaginative hopes of Black Americans.[259]

McGann notices that songs which speak truth about struggle seem to ease the burden of members of the congregation at Our Lady of Lourdes. Sometimes the lyrics of a song provide explicit encouragement. One member explained to her, "'You go through so much in a lifetime, and sometimes we run into problems... That song lets you know not to give up... Don't make it easier for me, but give me enough strength to make it over. That says a lot about life... You go *through* the challenges! That song says so much – just gives me the strength to keep going!'"[260] Sometimes, however, the act of singing itself allows the congregation to engage in "releasing... the very heartaches of which [they had] just sung."[261]

THE BONDING ROLE OF MUSIC IN SPIRITUALS AND GOSPEL SONGS

Often, the texts of these spirituals and gospels are set in the singular. Although whole congregations sing together, the lyrics state "I" and "me" rather than "we" and "us." As McGann noted in her study of the music of an African-American congregation, "lyrics of the gospel

---

[259] Ibid., 136.

[260] Ibid., 79. The song to which Carey Monroe refers is "Lord, Don't Move that Mountain;"
Lord, don't move that mountain, but give me strength to climb it!
Lord, don't take away my stumbling block, but lead me all around it!
The way may not be easy, you didn't say that it would be.
But when our tribulations get too light, we tend to stay away from
Thee.

[261] Ibid., 95.

songs sung at Lourdes have much in common with biblical psalms... Like their scriptural counterparts, they often speak in the voice of testimony, the first person singular, assuming, like the communities from which the psalm emerged, that the 'I' of song lyrics is deeply rooted in a communal identity of 'we'."[262] Part of the musical role of these songs, therefore, is to make words set in first person singular function as though they were in first person plural. The music to spirituals and gospel songs functions as a community builder; when sung to the syncopated, pentatonic, and repetitive melodies of spirituals and gospel songs, these texts take on a plural connotation. As stated earlier, spirituals arose out of heterophonic music-making, with individual variations in the performances of every voice in the congregation. There can be no heterophony without a plurality of singers, just as there can be no call-and-response. Spirituals and gospel songs achieve a full expression of their musicality only when many people sing together. Albert J. Raboteau highlights this communal function of spirituals in his history of the beginnings of the African-American Church, *Slave Religion:*

> The flexible, improvisational structure of the spirituals gave them the capacity to fit an individual slave's experience into the consciousness of the group. One person's sorrow or joy became everyone's through song. Singing the spirituals was therefore both an intensely personal and vividly communal experience in which an individual received consolation for sorrow and gained a heightening of joy because his experience was shared. Perhaps in the very structure of many spirituals one can see articulated this notion of communal support. In the pattern of overlapping call and response an individual would extemporize the verses, freely interjecting new ones from other spirituals. Frequently, before he was finished, everyone else would be repeating a chorus familiar to all. This pattern may be seen as a metaphor for the individual believer's relationship to the

---

[262] Ibid., 148. McGann notes, as mentioned earlier, that African-American Gospel music often makes use of the testimonial function described in Chapter 4.

community. His changing daily experience, like the verses improvised by the leader, was "based" by the constancy of his Christian community.[263]

Such communal sharing of each individual's sorrows and joys is not limited to the spirituals. We find this happening in the early Gospel songs of Tindley as well as in later Gospel music, such as that sung at Our Lady of Lourdes.

McGann also finds that the intentionally emotional nature of gospel music fosters communal engagement. She locates much of the emotional impact of the music in its "recurring buildup of tension and release," evident in the way volume is increased by layering voices and instruments and in the use of repeated vamps which "explode into a moment of release" when these patterns are finally exchanged for a new musical phrase. "Emotions are set in motion by this buildup of tension and release, emotions that draw members of the community beyond their personal realms of thought and self-awareness into a space of shared feeling and engagement."[264]

SCRIPTURAL UNDERSTANDING OF THE TRUTH-TELLING ROLE OF MUSIC

In recent years, worship leaders have paid more attention to the songs of lament found in the Bible. They have learned from Biblical scholars who point out that, of the various types or genres of Psalms found in the Bible, the largest number are individual complaints. When

---

[263] Raboteau, 246.

[264] McGann, 200-201.

172

added together with the communal complaints, this number totals one-third of the entire Psalter.[265] Such a proclivity of individual and communal psalms of lament, sometimes called complaint psalms, upholds the need for truth-telling about difficult situations during Christian worship.

These psalms provide a model for the lamentation and truth-telling of the spirituals and gospel songs. They use vivid language to express current suffering, as in Psalm 102: "For my days pass away like smoke, and my bones burn like a furnace. My heart is stricken and withered like grass; I am too wasted to eat my bread" (vs. 3-4). They can include blessings of God in the midst of trials, as in Psalm 22:3-5, an incongruity which reminds one of the "Glory, hallelujah" at the end of "Nobody Knows the Trouble I've Seen." They often acknowledge that only God can redeem people, as in Psalm 51: "Purge me with hyssop, and I shall be clean... Create in me a clean heart, O God" (vs. 7, 10). This recognition of God as the source of all help mirrors the emphasis on needing prayer in the spirituals. Further, the trials of the ancient Israelites, lamented in the psalms, provided a precedent and a model for the African-American slaves in understanding their suffering and crafting their musical responses.[266]

The scriptures are likewise full of examples of truth-telling that takes the form of protest. The prophets of the Hebrew Bible often spoke courageously in the face of wrong-doing and disregard for God's will. They understood their bold prophecies as the fulfilling of God's call upon

---

[265] Erhard S. Gerstenberger, *Psalms: Part 1: with an Introduction to Cultic Poetry* (Grand Rapids: Eerdmans, 1988), 14, 245.

[266] See Wilma Ann Bailey, "The Sorrow Songs: Laments from the Old Testament and African American Experience," in *Music in Christian Worship: At the Service of the Liturgy*, ed. Charlotte Kroeker (Collegeville, Minnesota: Liturgical Press, 2005), 75-82.

their lives (Jeremiah 1:5); they overturned the people's assumptions that worship rituals are more important that just and equitable living (Isaiah 1:11-17); they called the people around them to repentance, matching the vehemence of their exhortations with the tenderness of their descriptions of God's mercy (Joel 2:12-14); and they proclaimed that God shall have the final word (Obadiah 15-17). Creators and singers of spirituals and gospel songs could look to these prophets of long ago and imitate their faith and their bravery in protest of contemporary situations.

Other Biblical figures turn their forthright speech to God rather than to the people around them. Job has often served as the prime example of someone of faith who dares to confront God with the painful realities of his life. While his friends insist that he must have sinned and thus earned the disaster which befell him, Job dares to "speak in the anguish of [his] spirit... complain in the bitterness of [his] soul" to God (7:11). And while God may not answer Job's questions in the way he had hoped, neither does the Almighty punish him for asking in the first place. Job's direct questioning of God is seen in other scriptural pericopes as well. Abraham dares to argue with God about the number of righteous people the Lord requires in order to refrain from destroying the city of Sodom (Genesis 18:23-33). Jacob, in a passage mentioned in an earlier chapter of this work, actually wrestles with God, insisting on a blessing, which he receives with an unexpected wound (Genesis 32:22-32). Even Jesus, in agony on the cross, borrows words from a Psalm in order to ask why God has abandoned him (Mark 15:34). We find models of truth-telling to the Creator as well as to the culture in these examples of scripture. Spirituals echo this bare honesty. Thomas Dorsey, writing just after the death of his wife and infant son during childbirth, penned the heart-felt cry to God: "I am tired, I am weak, I am worn... at the river I stand, guide my feet, hold my hand."[267] Likewise, Charles Albert Tindley could confront the realities of aging when addressing his Maker:

> When I'm growing old and feeble, stand by me.
> When I'm growing old and feeble, stand by me.
> When my life becomes a burden, and I'm nearing chilly Jordan,
> O thou Lily of the Valley, stand by me.[268]

CRITICISM OF SPIRITUALS, GOSPEL MUSIC, AND TRUTH-TELLING SONGS

There is a large gulf between the numbers of Americans who appreciate or enjoy spirituals and gospel songs and the numbers of those who sing them regularly in worship. With other styles of music covered in this work, complaint or critique of a genre typically implies dislike of the musical style, theological content, or another facet of that body of music. But African-American worship music presents an interesting contrast. If people like spirituals and gospels, why aren't they sung more often in worship, particularly among white congregations?

A large part of the answer to this question lies in the deep connections between the music and the culture of origin of spirituals and gospel songs. Non-reformed congregations do not hesitate to use Genevan psalm tunes in worship, especially Old Hundredth, the melody for the Doxology. Non-Methodist congregations borrow freely from the texts of Charles Wesley without any guilt or embarrassment. And people of all languages sing "Silent Night" at Christmas time, not

---

[267] Thomas A. Dorsey, "Precious Lord, Take My Hand," in *The United Methodist Hymnal* (Nashville: The United Methodist Publishing House, 1989), 474.

[268] Charles Albert Tindley, "Stand by Me," in *The United Methodist Hymnal*, 512.

worrying that they aren't German enough to sing the hymn well. Yet white congregations, faced with music from the African-American tradition, often shy away out of fears that the white use of black music might be disrespectful or inauthentic.

Such fears are not entirely ungrounded. There is a long history of disrespectful appropriation of African-American music, from the mocking minstrel shows mentioned above to the highly edited, Europeanized versions of spirituals published in the nineteenth and twentieth centuries. Although the latter were often issued with good intentions, they unfortunately bastardized the songs they sought to transmit, cutting them away from the very musical elements that constituted authentic African-American music. Even today, assumptions about the printing and performance of African-American music abound. Hymnal editors struggle to provide fitting notation for an art form that arose in an oral and aural culture. Choirs that sing arrangements of spirituals wonder about the incorporation of movement, hand-clapping, and foot-stomping into their performance. Choir directors might translate the "energy" associated with African-American music into quick tempos, regardless of the content of the lyrics or the musical nature of the melody. Meanwhile, performers and audiences alike are left wondering, "is this authentic?" Inauthentic performance or use is often equated with disrespect for the music and the culture, and many congregations, choirs, and directors seem to find it safer to avoid spirituals and gospels rather than chance offending with a less-than-faithful rendition.

The question of how frequently spirituals are sung in African-American congregations also deserves some investigation. Scholar Melva Wilson Costen briefly explores the substitution of choir performances of contemporary gospel songs for congregational singing of hymns and spirituals in her study of music in African-American

176

churches, *In Spirit and In Truth*. She finds that "some of the carefully honed African American historical folk theology with reminders of God at work in the common struggles and rewards of unified social efforts are omitted from the good news" being sung today in many African-American congregations.[269] As new music makes its way into the repertoire of these churches, older songs, including the spirituals, often give way. Costen points out that the gospel choir, with its repertoire of concertized gospel arrangements, seems to be replacing congregation singing of hymns and spirituals in many congregations. Wyatt Tee Walker closes his study of "Black sacred music and social change" with a charge to retain historic gospel songs and spirituals: "The Black Church of the future must seriously and systematically preserve, develop, and utilize this rich resource if it is to engage in service commensurate with both its past history and its future challenges."[270]

Another critique pertains more closely to the function of truth-telling in worship discussed in this chapter. There seems to be an unwritten rule of positivity in Christian worship. Congregations and their leaders often resist the inclusion of lament, sorrow, complaint, or protest in worship. This is amply evidenced by the loss of the prayer of confession in many congregations, by the overwhelmingly joyful tenor of most congregational singing, and by the hesitation that many seem to feel when bringing their own sorrow to church. Stories of people who feel unwelcome in worship after living through dark days abound. Why is this?

---

[269] Melva Wilson Costen, *In Spirit and In Truth: The Music of African American Worship* (Louisville: Westminster John Knox, 2004), 72.

[270] Walker, 193.

Like Job's friends, many Christians believe, consciously or otherwise, that God rewards those of strong faith with good lives. Such belief implies that those who face trials and sorrows must have somehow earned them. Although this "prosperity gospel" isn't explicitly advocated by many congregations, it is such an indelible part of the American culture that its effects are hard to eradicate. In the face of the prosperity gospel, those who come to worship with broken spirits and sad faces are opening themselves to the assumptions of others concerning how they may have "earned" such misfortune. Those already suffering may simply find it less painful to avoid worship and these assumptions.

Another reason behind the abundance of positivity in worship music is the way congregations understand the function of music at church. If the purpose of music is to praise God, lamentation will understandably be left out. If music is to share testimonies that can lead to the conversion of others, protest and complaint will be eliminated as not attractive enough to lure unbelievers. And if music allows us to respond to the scriptures and prayers of the worship service, then such music will not make room for truth-telling unless the stories of pain and loss in the Bible are read, stories that might well be edited out of lectionaries (whether formal ecumenical or *ad hoc* ones created by a particular pastor's sermon series). So few traditions value a time of honest expression of anger, sorrow, or complaint that music that serves these purposes is often kept out of worship.

INTRODUCING THIS FUNCTION INTO THE WORSHIP OF OTHER TRADITIONS

Recently, many scholars of worship have expressed the desire to reclaim the traditions of lamentation and other forms of truth-telling

178

in communal worship.[271] Awareness of these "lost language[s]," to use one author's phrase, has reached the congregational level as well, and many churches, whole denominations as well as individual congregations, have wrestled with ways to incorporate Biblical models of lament in their worship. We will explore two options available to worship leaders who seek to open up space in worship for singing songs of loss, sorrow, protest, and complaint.

Many congregations, when recognizing a need to express feelings that might seem too negative for "normal" worship, have developed special services entirely dedicated to this purpose. Those who find holiday celebrations dampened by grief over the death of loved ones can attend "Blue Christmas" services. Also called "Longest Night" services, these times of worship offer those who suffer from grief or other pain the opportunity to bring their troubles into dialogue with the Christmas story. These times of worship can be a needed respite from the forced jollity of the days surrounding Christmas. Although one of the earliest versions of this service did not contain any African-American music, (see www.rockies.net/~spirit/sermons/bluexmas.php), one can easily identify songs from this tradition to allow a grieving people to lift up their pain to God. "Goin' Up Yonder"

---

[271] See Matthew Boulton, "Forsaking God: a theological argument for Christian Lamentation," in *Scottish Journal of Theology*, 2002, Vol. 55, 58-78; Stephen Breck Reid, "Laments and Worship," in *Clergy Journal*, Nov 2005, Vol. 82, #2, 8-9; William L. Holladay, "Songs for Christians: Using the Whole Psalter," in *Christian Century*, January 5, 1994, Vol 111, #1, 12-14; Dwight Vogel, "Cutting Edges," in *Clergy Journal*, October 2002, Vol 79, #1, 19-20; Michael Card, *A Sacred Sorrow: Reaching out to God in the Lost Language of Lament* (Colorado Springs: NavPress, 2005); Reggie Kidd, *With One Voice: Discovering Christ's Song in our Worship* (Grand Rapids: Baker, 2005); Debra and Ron Rienstra, *Worship Words: Disciplining Language for Faithful Ministry* (Grand Rapids: Baker, 2009); Paul Bradbury, *Sowing in Tears: How to Lament in a Church of Praise* (Cambridge: Grove, 2007); and Ruth Snyder Miller, "Weeping in Worship: Collaborative Preaching on Texts of Lament," (D.Min thesis: Columbia Theological Seminary, 2003), among others.

highlights the eschatological aspects of the Advent season while reflecting truthfully on the heartache inherent in human life:

> I can take the pain, the heartaches they bring,
> the comfort's there in knowing I'll soon be gone.
> As God gives me grace, I'll run this race,
> until I see my savior face to face.[272]

The same sentiments are found in Charles Tindley's great song of grief and hope:

> Burdens now may crush me down,
> disappointments all around,
> troubles speak in mournful sigh,
> sorrow through a tear-stained eye;
> there is a world where pleasure reigns,
> no mourning soul shall roam its plains,
> and to that land of peace and glory
> I want to go someday.[273]

Lift Every Voice and Sing II, the African-American hymnal published by the Episcopal Church, even recommends "Swing Low, Sweet Chariot" as an Advent hymn; this familiar text and comforting melody provide yet another opportunity to admit weakness and sorrow while not entirely giving way to despair.

Other occasions besides Christmas exist for services dedicated to truth-telling in word and song. The days before Easter, Holy Week and in particular the Triduum of Maundy Thursday, Good Friday, and Holy Saturday, also provide an opportunity to allow individuals to grieve and lament while the whole church pauses at the solemn death of Christ. Unlike at Blue Christmas, on this occasion mourners and those

---

[272] Walter Hawkins, © 1976 Bud John Music, Inc. (Admin. by Capitol CMG Publishing) Used with permission.

[273] Charles A. Tindley, "Some Day," in *Zion Still Sings*, 139.

facing particular difficulties will be in the majority, as many Christians finish their Lenten fasts and focus on the somber recollection of Christ's death. African-American spirituals and gospel songs provide a wealth of material that commemorates the passion of Christ while allowing room for individual complaint as well. "Jesus Walked this Lonesome Valley," "He Never Said a Mumbalin' Word," "Were You There When They Crucified My Lord," and "I Want Jesus to Walk with Me," testify to the powerful way in which the spiritual allows scriptural testimony, public worship, and personal pain to intermingle so fruitfully and truthfully.

Just as many congregations have made Blue Christmas services available to the community of grieving people around them, likewise many congregations are recognizing the need for a liturgical response to physical pain and sickness. Healing services have been appearing more and more frequently in the repertoire of congregational responses to the worship needs of their members and others. These are opportunities for truth-telling about the exhaustion and pain of combating illness, as well as chances to admit our need for God's help and our desire for healing. Worship leaders must be careful to define healing broadly, making room for rescue from physical illness but recognizing that human prayers cannot force God to act in a particular way.

Spirituals and gospel songs that could provide comfort and release at healing services abound. An African-American hymnal published by the United Methodist Church, *Zion Still Sings*, contains a section of songs recommended for occasions of healing, including the familiar "There is a Balm" as well as the less well-known "Come on in My Room:"

Come on in ma room.
Oh, come on in ma room.
Oh, Jesus is ma doctor
And he writes down all ma scriptions
And he gives me all of my medicines in ma room.[274]

Other appropriate pieces include "Do Lord, Remember Me," "Kum Bah-Ya," and "Fix Me, Jesus."

Some congregations may choose, however, to integrate lamentation and protest into their worship services more frequently. They may see the benefits of whole services dedicated to grieving during the holidays or prayers for healing, but they may also wish to include truth-telling as a regular component in weekly worship. There are several ideal locations within the Sunday service for the congregation to sing its complaints and protests to God.

The first of these might be during the prayer of confession. Although eliminated from many congregations' worship diets by worship leaders' fear of causing offence, the prayer of confession is a wonderful occasion to be honest with God and neighbor. In the prayer of confession, we truthfully admit that we, like Paul, do not do what we want, but instead do the evil that we wish we wouldn't do. In making this confession, we free ourselves to receive forgiveness from our Lord. A familiar song such as "Standing in the Need of Prayer" could open a time of confession for the congregation by helping each one to admit and sing aloud that we all need prayer.

Another opportunity for musical truth-telling comes during the congregation's time of prayer. This prayer time has, in some congregations, devolved into an exceedingly brief petition that the

---

[274] "Come On in My Room," in *Zion Still Sings*, 118. Copyright held by Cecilia Clemons. Used with permission.

congregation would receive blessings from God and would put into action the words spoken during the sermon. But some congregations use this time of prayer to lift up both personal and global concerns. When congregation members understand their connection through the Body of Christ to Christians on every continent, and when they believe in God's love for all people, then they can be motivated by God's compassion to pray for victims of natural disasters, ethnic strife, and unjust political systems around the world, among other things. Amid such petitions, it seems appropriate to offer up prayers of protest. The same songs that sustained people of faith during the civil rights movement in this country might again be lifted to God in protest at continuing lethal violence between Palestinians and Israelis, the violation of human rights in China, or the countless deaths due to AIDS in Africa and elsewhere. In the face of such tragedies, "Go Down, Moses" and "We Shall Overcome" both offer honest prayers to God of a desire for change, and energize the congregation to do its part in extending God's steadfast love to all people.

Having investigated six different genres of worship music and searched for their connections to particular functions within the worship service, we ought to remind ourselves of the limitations as well as the benefits of linking style and function when seeking to understand the Church's worship and music. We will also turn to the question of what the outcomes of such a study might or should be.

CHAPTER 8: CONCLUSIONS TO THE STUDY EXAMINING THE REASONS WHY WE SING

A college I once visited wanted to honor the various religious traditions of its students. Within the college chapel, a building which testified to the Christian origins of the college, the administration hung colorful banners symbolizing seven different faith traditions. While the intended purpose of the banners was to honor these different religions, the method of doing so seemed, to me, somewhat demeaning. The banners were identical in size and shape, hung in rows from the vaulted ceiling of the chapel in such a way that they seemed interchangeable and entirely similar. Yet these faiths have crucial differences, different ways of understanding the world and relating to God that the banners glossed over rather than expressed.

When we assume that different genres of church music are all the same, that the only thing that separates them are our preferences for one style over another, we slight the worth of each one. We do not honor various traditions by ignoring what makes them unique, but by coming to understand them in their individuality. I have attempted to encourage deeper glimpses into the particular histories and strengths and ways of functioning within worship of each musical genre included in this book. My research and writing arises out of a deep regard for particular songs, hymns, composers, performers, and personal experiences affiliated with every musical tradition discussed. While my experience with each tradition is different (some genres surrounded me from birth, some I have met more recently), I believe there is material worthy of study and singing in each of the genres mentioned.

Yet this book presents a contradiction as well. Each chapter closes with suggestions for those who might want to incorporate both the function and some examples of each musical tradition into their worship services. Such an inclusive stance has much to commend it. As I wrote in the Introduction, I think that by including different musical traditions within a congregation's worshipping practice, and therefore attending to different functions of music for worship, the members of the congregation gradually come to a broader understanding and experience of God. Carried to a logical, however distant, conclusion, such an argument would advocate that all worship services should include examples from all musical traditions, eventually resulting in congregations which all worship with the same, eclectic palette of Global songs, Taizé chants, Contemporary Christian Music ballads, Lutheran chorales, metrical psalms, Gospel songs, African-American spirituals, and so on. Such an outcome, as difficult as it might be to imagine, would eradicate the very traditions that this book seeks to explore and honor.

While I believe that many congregations would benefit from exposure to a variety of styles and traditions of music, I do not seek to force all congregations to give up their stylistic purity. The world would be poorer without faithful African-American congregations, large and small, drenching their Sunday prayers in a flood of spirituals and Gospel music, contemporary and historic. The stylistic purity of Taizé prayers, sung in quiet devotion, is a blessing. Even the contemporary song set, much as some of my colleagues in the field of liturgical music may prefer to deny this, when constructed and led with prayerful attention to God and to the congregation, may be a thing of great beauty and great power.

I do not wish to deny adherents to particular traditions the ability to worship in "stylistic purity." Yet neither do I believe it to be beneficial to worship "as we've always done" (whether "always" signifies five years or five hundred years) without examining *how* one's congregation has arrived at such a musical and liturgical form of worship, *what* such worship (and in particular the singing included in

185

this worship) intends to do, and *why* other congregations, denominations, and cultures find other worship music beautiful and beneficial.

Such an examination, toward which I hope that this book may prove a helpful beginning, might well bring one home again with a renewed respect for one's own traditions, but with a new-found understanding of the different genres of music sung by Christians today, each with its own function and charm. Then again, the process of examining the various styles of music in the Church may lead one to wish to explore one or more of these styles further, or to begin singing them in worship along with what is already familiar. I hope that such a process may bring us all to sing with our spirit, but also with our understanding, as Paul urges the Christians in Corinth (1 Cor 14:15). Here, understanding (or intellect) and spirit (or passion) are not at odds with one another, but are complementary in together allowing the Christian to sing holistically, with heart and mind and soul.

In particular, I hope that this book may be of benefit to those who lead the Body of Christ in song week after week. Understanding what a congregation expects its music to accomplish in worship is a critical task for all who seek to lead the people of God in worship and in song. The ideas presented here are necessarily generalizations, but it is hoped that they will be helpful ones: ideas that encourage congregations and their leaders to ask "What do we assume music in worship is for?" and "Are there other roles that music can or should serve?" May God bless those who seek to understand more deeply the worship to which all God's children are called.

BIBLIOGRAPHY

American Academy of Religion. *The HarperCollins Dictionary of Religion.* Edited by Jonathan Z. Smith and William Scott Green. New York: HarperOne, 1995.

Anderson, E. Byron. *Worship and Christian Identity: Practicing Ourselves.* Collegeville, MN: Liturgical Press, 2003.

Ateliers et Presses de Taizé. "Meditative Singing." Taizé. Last modified July 27, 2004. Accessed June 25, 2012. http://www.taize.fr/en_article338.html.

Ateliers et Presses de Taizé. "The Value of Silence." Taizé. Last modified October 24, 2001. Accessed June 28, 2010. http://www.taize.fr/en_article12.html.

Basden, Paul A., ed. *Exploring the Worship Spectrum.* Grand Rapids: Zondervan, 2004.

Beaujon, Andrew. *Body Piercing Saved My Life: Inside the Phenomenon of Christian Rock.* Cambridge, MA: Da Capo, 2006.

Best, Harold. *Music through the Eyes of Faith.* San Francisco: Harper, 1993.

Black, George. "Church Musician in France: Part II Canons at Taizé." *The American Organist,* July 1980.

Boulton, Matthew. "Forsaking God: A Theological Argument for Christian Lamentation." *Scottish Journal of Theology* 55 (2002): 58-78.

Bradbury, Paul. *Sowing in Tears: How to Lament in a Church of Praise.* Cambridge: Grove, 2007.

Bradley, Patricia. *Making American Culture: A Social History, 1900-1920.* Basingstoke, Hampshire: Palgrave Macmillan, 2009.

Bradshaw, Paul F., Maxwell E. Johnson, and L. Edward Phillips. *The Apostolic Constitution: A Commentary.* Minneapolis: Fortress Press, 2002.

Bradshaw, Paul. *Reconstructing Early Christian Worship.* Collegeville: Liturgical Press, 2010.

Brink, Emily R., and Bert Polman, eds. *Psalter Hymnal Handbook.* Grand Rapids: CRC Publications, 1998.

Brown, Frank Burch. *Inclusive Yet Discerning: Navigating Worship Artfully.* Grand Rapids: Eerdmans, 2009.

Calvin, John. "Foreword to the Genevan Psalter." In *Source Readings in Music History*, edited and translated by Oliver Strunk. New York: Norton, 1950.

Card, Michael. *A Sacred Sorrow: Reaching out to God in the Lost Language of Lament.* Colorado Springs: NavPress, 2005.

Cartledge, Mark J. *Encountering the Spirit: The Charismatic Tradition.* London: Darton, Longman and Tood, 2006.

Chrysostom, John. "Exposition of Psalm XLI." In *Source Readings in Music History*, edited by Oliver Strunk. New York: Norton, 1950.

Cone, James H. *The Spirituals and the Blues: An Interpretation.* New York: Seabury Press, 1972.

"Constitution on the Sacred Liturgy Sacrosanctum Concilium." The Holy See. Accessed May 31, 2010. http://www.vatican.va/archive/hist_councils/ ii_vatican_council/documents/vat- ii_const_19631204_sacrosanctum-concilium_en.html.

Costen, Melva Wilson. *African-American Christian Worship.* Nashville: Abingdon Press, 1993.

_____. *In Spirit and in Truth: The Music of African American Worship.* Louisville: Westminster John Knox, 2004.

Cross, F. L., and E. A. Livingstone, eds. *The Oxford Dictionary of the Christian Church.* 3rd rev. ed. New York: Oxford University Press, 2005.

Darden, Robert. *People Get Ready! A New History of Black Gospel Music.* New York: Continuum, 2004.

Davidson, James Robert. *A Dictionary of Protestant Church Music.* Metuchen, NJ: Scarecrow Press, 1975.

Deiss, Lucien. *Springtime of the Liturgy.* Translated by Matthew J. O'Connell. Collegeville, MN: Liturgical Press, 1979.

189

Eskew, Harry, and Hugh T. McElrath. *Sing with Understanding: An Introduction to Christian Hymnology.* Nashville: Church Street Press, 1995.

The Faith We Sing. Singer's ed. Nashville: Abingdon Press, 2000.

The Fight of My Life. Performed by Kirk Franklin. Gospo Centric, 2007, compact disc.

Franklin, Kirk. "Someone Asked the Question" (No. 2144) in *The Faith We Sing.* Nashville: Abingdon Press, 2000.

General Board of Church and Society. "Social Principles." General Board of Church and Society of the United Methodist Church. Last modified 2015. Accessed September 7, 2011. http://umc-gbcs.org/social-principles.

Gerstenberger, Erhard S. *Psalms Part I, with an Introduction to Cultic Poetry.* Edited by Rolf Knierim and Gene M. Tucker. Vol. 14 of *The Forms of Old Testament Literature.* Grand Rapids: Eerdmans, 1988.

Goldstein, Niles Elliot, ed. *Spiritual Manifestos: Visions for Renewed Religious Life in America from Young Spiritual Leaders of Many Faiths.* Woodstock, VT: Skylight Paths Publishing, 1999.

Harper, John. *The Forms and Orders of Western Liturgy from the Tenth to the Eighteenth Century.* New York: Clarendon Press, 1991.

Hawn, C. Michael. *Gather into One: Praying and Singing Globally.* Grand Rapids: Eerdmans, 2003.

Hawn, C. Michael. *New Songs of Celebration Render: Congregational Song in the Twenty-First Century.* Chicago: GIA, 2013.

Hawn, C. Michael. "Streams of Song: An Overview of Congregational Song in the Twenty-First Century." *The Hymn* 61, no. 1 (Winter 2010): 16-26.

Hello Fear. Performed by Kirk Franklin. Gospo Centric, 2001, compact disc.

Herring, Brad. *Sound, Lighting, and Video: A Resource for Worship.* New York: Focal Press, 2009.

Holladay, William L. "Songs for Christians: Using the Whole Psalter."
Christian Century 111, no. 1 (January 5, 1994): 12-14.

Hotz, Kendra G., and Matthew T. Mathews. *Shaping the Christian Life:
Worship and the Religious Affections.* Louisville: Westminster
John Knox Press, 2006.

"I Am a Friend of God." Accessed June 6, 2012.
http://www.lyricsmode.com/lyrics/i/
israel_houghton/i_am_a_friend_of_god.html.

Janco, Steven R. "From Stylistic Stalemate to Focus on Function." *Liturgy*
24, no. 4 (2009): 48-54.

Jasper, R. C. D., and G. J. Cumming, eds. *Prayers of the Eucharist: Early and
Reformed.* New York: Oxford University Press, 1980.

Johnson, Charles A. *The Frontier Camp Meeting: Religion's Harvest Time.*
Dallas: Southern Methodist University Press, 1955.

Johnson, Todd E., ed. *The Conviction of Things Not Seen: Currents in
Protestant Christianity in the Twenty-First Century.* Grand
Rapids: Brazos Press, 2002.

Jones, Cheslyn, Geoffrey Wainwright, Edward Yarnold, and Paul
Bradshaw, eds. *The Study of Liturgy.* Rev. ed. New York: Oxford
University Press, 1992.

Jones, Tony. *The Sacred Way: Spiritual Practices for Everyday Life.* Grand
Rapids: Zondervan, 2005.

Joseph, Mark. *The Rock and Roll Rebellion.* Nashville: Broadman and
Holman, 1999.

Jungmann, Joseph A. *The Mass of the Roman Rite: Its Origins and
Development.* translated by Francis A. Brunner. Vol. 1. Allen, TX:
Christian Classics, 1986. First published 1951 by Benziger
Brothers.

Kay, William K., and Anne E. Dyer, eds. *Pentecostal and Charismatic
Studies: A Reader.* London: SCM Press, 2004.

Kidd, Reggie. *With One Voice: Discovering Christ's Song in Our Worship.*
Grand Rapids: Baker, 2005.

Kittel, Gerhard, and Gerhard Friedrich, eds. *Theological Dictionary of the
New Testament.* Grand Rapids: Eerdmans, 1968.

Kroeker, Charlotte, ed. *Music in Christian Worship: At the Service of the Liturgy.* Collegeville, MN: Liturgical Press, 2005.

Kropf, Marlene, and Kenneth Nafziger. *Singing: A Mennonite Voice.* Scottdale, PA: Herald Press, 2001.

Kubicki, Judith Marie. *Liturgical Music as Ritual Symbol: A Case Study of Jacques Berthier's Taizé Music.* Leuven, Belgium: Peeters, 1999.

Lathrop, Gordon. *Holy Ground: A Liturgical Cosmology.* Minneapolis: Fortress Press, 2003.

London, Herbert I. *Closing the Circle: A Cultural History of the Rock Revolution.* Chicago: Nelson-Hall, 1984.

Luther, Martin. *Liturgy and Hymns.* Edited by Ulrich S. Leupold, Jeroslav Pelikan, and Helmut T. Lehmann. Translated by Paul Zeller Strodach. American ed. Vol. 53 of *Luther's Works.* Philadelphia: Fortress, 1965.

McCart, Thomas K. *The Matter and Manner of Praise: The Controversial Evolution of Hymnody in the Church of England 1760-1820.* Lanham, MD: Scarecrow Press, 1998.

McGann, Mary E. *A Precious Fountain: Music in the Worship of an African-American Catholic Community.* Collegeville, MN: Liturgical Press, 2004.

Miller, Ruth Snyder. "Weeping in Worship: Collaborative Preaching on Texts of Lament." Doctoral thesis, Columbia Theological Seminary, 2003.

Miller, Terry E., and Andrew Shahriari. *World Music: A Global Journey.* 2nd ed. New York: Routledge, 2006.

Missa Luba: Mass in Congolese Style for Mixed Chorus with Tenor Soloist and Percussion. New York: Lawson-Gould Music Publishers, 1964.

Missouri Synod, Accessed June 23, 2010. http://www.lcms.org/pages/internal.asp?NavID=708.

Moore, Allan, ed. *The Cambridge Companion to Blues and Gospel Music.* New York: Cambridge University Press, 2002.

Murphy, Troy A. "Rhetorical Invention and the Transformation of 'We Shall Overcome.'" *Qualitative Research Reports in Communication* 4 (2003): 1-8.

Music, David W., ed. *Hymnody: A Collection of Source Readings.* Lanham, MD: Scarecrow Press, 1996.

Page, Nick. *And Now Let's Move into a Time of Nonsense: Why Worship Songs Are Failing the Church.* Waynesboro, GA: Authentic, 2004.

Parker, Alice. *Melodious Accord: Good Singing in the Church.* Chicago: Liturgy Training Publications, 1991.

Paroissien Romain. Tournai, Belgium: Desclée et Cie, 1931.

Pinson, J. Matthew, ed. *Perspectives on Christian Worship: 5 Views.* Nashville: B&H Academic, 2009.

The Praise and Worship Fake Book. Franklin, TN: Brentwood-Benson, 2003.

Psalter Hymnal. Grand Rapids: CRC Publications, 1987.

Raboteau, Albert J. *Slave Religion: The "Invisible Institution" in the Antebellum South.* New York: Oxford University Press, 1978.

Rahner, Karl, Cornelius Ernst, and Kevin Smyth, eds. *Sacramentum Mundi: An Encyclopedia of Theology.* New York: Herder & Herder, 1969.

Redman, Robb. *The Great Worship Awakening: Singing a New Song in the Postmodern Church.* San Francisco: Jossey-Bass, 2002.

Reformed Church in America. "Confession of Belhar." RCA: Reformed Church in America. Last modified 2015. Accessed September 7, 2011. http://www.rca.org/sslpage.aspx?pid=304.

Reid, Stephen Breck. "Laments and Worship." *Clergy Journal* 82, no. 2 (November 2005): 8-9.

Rienstra, Debra, and Ron Rienstra. *Worship Words: Disciplining Language for Faithful Ministry.* Grand Rapids: Baker, 2009.

Rejoice in the Lord. Grand Rapids: Eerdmans Publishing Company, 1985.

Roof, Wade Clark, ed. *Contemporary American Religion.* New York: Macmillan Reference, 1999.

Routley, Erik. *Music Leadership in the Church.* Nashville: Abingdon Press, 1967.

Routley, Erik. *A Panorama of Christian Hymnody.* Edited by Paul A. Richardson. Chicago: GIA Publications, 2005.

Saliers, Don. *Worship and Spirituality.* Akron, OH: OSL Publications, 1992.

Santos, Jason Brian. *A Community Called Taizé: A Story of Prayer, Worship, and Reconciliation.* Downers Grove, IL: IVP Books, 2008.

Schalk, Carl. *Luther on Music: Paradigms of Praise.* St. Louis: Concordia, 1988.

Sendry, Alfred. *Music in Ancient Israel.* New York: Philosophical Library, 1969.

Sing to the Lord: Music in Divine Worship. Washington, DC: United States Conference of Catholic Bishops, 2007.

Smith, David. *The Biography of Rev. David Smith.* Xenia, OH, 1881.

Smith, William S. *Joyful Noise: A Guide to Music in the Church for Pastors and Musicians.* Franklin, TN: Providence House Publishers, 2007.

Songs and Prayers of Taizé. Chicago: GIA Publications, 1991.

Stapert, Calvin R. *A New Song for an Old World: Musical Thought in the Early Church.* Grand Rapids: Eerdmans, 2007.

Stiller, Gunther. *Johann Sebastian Bach and Liturgical Life in Leipzig.* Translated by Herber J. A. Bouman, Daniel F. Poellot, and Hilton C. Oswald. St. Louis: Concordia, 1984.

Strasburger, Victor C. *Adolescents and the Media: Medical and Psychological Impact.* Thousand Oaks, CA: SAGE Publications, 1995.

Tillich, Paul. *Dynamics of Faith.* New York: Harper & Brothers Publishers, 1957.

Tomaine, Jane. *St. Benedict's Toolbox: The Nuts and Bolts of Everyday Benedictine Living.* Harrisburg, PA: Morehouse, 2005.

Tood, Neil P. McAngus, and Frederick W. Cody. "Vestibular Responses to Loud Dance Music: A Physiological Basis of the 'Rock and Roll

Threshold'?" *Journal of the Acoustical Society of America*, 107 (January 2000): 499.

Troeger, Thomas H. *Wonder Reborn: Creating Sermons on Hymns, Music, and Poetry.* New York: Oxford University Press, 2010.

The United Methodist Hymnal. Nashville: United Methodist Publishing House, 1989.

Van Pelt, Doug. "The Ugly Truth Behind Christian Rock." *HM: The Hard Music Magazine.* November/December 2003, 38.

Vogel, Dwight. "Cutting Edges." *Clergy Journal* 79, no. 1 (October 2002): 19-20.

Wainwright, Geoffrey, and Karen B. Westerfield Tucker, eds. *The Oxford History of Christian Worship.* New York: Oxford University Press, 2006.

Walker, Wyatt Tee. *Somebody's Calling My Name: Black Sacred Music and Social Change.* Valley Forge, PA: Judson Press, 1992.

Warden, Michael D., ed. *Experience God in Worship.* Loveland, CO: Group Publishing, 2000.

Watts, Isaac. *The Psalms of David Imitated in the Language of the New Testament, in Hymnology: A Collection of Source Readings.* Edited by David Music. Lanham, MD: Scarecrow Press, 1996.

Watts, Isaac. *'Twas on That Dark, That Doleful Night.* Accessed September 27, 2012. http://www.hymnary.org/text/twas_on_that_dark_that_doleful_night.

Webber, Robert. *Worship Is a Verb.* Waco, TX: Word Books, 1985.

Westermeyer, Paul. *The Church Musician.* 2nd ed. Minneapolis: Augsburg Fortress Press, 1997.

Westermeyer, Paul. *Te Deum: The Church and Music.* Minneapolis: Fortress Press, 1998.

White, James F. *Protestant Worship: Traditions in Transition.* Louisville: Westminster John Knox Press, 1989.

"Who We Are." *CCLI.* Last modified 2014. Accessed June 21, 2010. http://www.ccli.com/WhoWeAre/.

Wilson-Dickson, Andrew. *The Story of Christian Music.* Paperback ed. Minneapolis: Fortress Press, 2003.

Winter, Miriam Therese, *Why Sing? Toward a Theology of Catholic Church Music.* Washington, DC: Pastoral Press, 1984.

Woods, Robert, and Brian Walrath, eds. *The Message in the Music: Studying Contemporary Praise and Worship.* Nashville: Abingdon Press, 2007.

Young, Carlton R. *Companion to the United Methodist Hymnal.* Nashville: Abingdon Press, 1993.

Young, Carlton R. *Music of the Heart: John and Charles Wesley on Music and Musicians.* Carol Stream, IL: Hope Publishing, 1995.

Young, Carlton R. *My Great Redeemer's Praise: An Introduction to Christian Hymns.* Akron: OSL Publications, 1995.

Zion Still Sings. Nashville: Abingdon Press, 2007.

INDEX OF NAMES